THEOLOGY OF THE BODY

for Teens

DISCOVERING GOD'S PLAN FOR LOVE AND LIFE

MIDDLE SCHOOL EDITION

Leader's Guide

Brian Butler, Jason Evert,
and Colin & Aimee MacIver

ASCENSION PRESS

West Chester, Pennsylvania

Nihil obstat: Dr. Christopher Baglow
           Censor Deputatus
           March 2, 2011

Imprimatur: +Most Reverend Gregory M. Aymond
           Archbishop of New Orleans
           March 2, 2011

Ascension Press
Post Office Box 1990
West Chester, PA 19380
Orders: 1-800-376-0520
www.AscensionPress.com

Cover design: Devin Schadt

Printed in the United States of America

ISBN: 978-1-935940-06-7

This book is dedicated to our loving parents, who have faithfully guided and prayerfully supported us over the years: Bob and Sheila Butler, Sam and Janie Evert, Bob MacIver, Kristine Sletten MacIver, and Eddie and Sue Boudreaux.

ACKNOWLEDGMENTS

We would like to thank the following people whose support and encouragement helped bring this project to fruition:

- **Archbishop Gregory M. Aymond**, for his encouragement and availability in helping us spread the message of the Theology of the Body to young people.

- **Dr. Christopher T. Baglow**, for his sharp theological critique and continued friendship.

- **Monica Ashour**, for sharing her wisdom and experience regarding the TOB and its connection with middle schoolers as we prepared the program.

- **Roch Gernon**, whose ideas and support helped us gain momentum in framing the structure of the program.

- The administration of **Saint Scholastica Academy**, whose support allowed (and continues to allow) Colin and Aimee the time to share the TOB message with others.

- The entire ministry team at **Dumb Ox Productions**, whose prayers, collaboration, experience, and creative gifts greatly enhanced this project.

- **Jen Messing,** whose thoughts and insights were helpful in improving the program.

- The many great reviewers whose suggestions contributed to the program: Mary Ann Chezik, Matt Chominski, Mark Ciesielski, Kevin Czarnecki, Very Reverend John Doerfler, Lisa Garcia, Shirley and Arthur Dupre, Jennifer Haggerty, Meaghan Hildebrandt, Lynn Pesce, and Roy Petitfils.

- **Lisa Butler**, for her loving support, incredible patience, and Southern hospitality at planning many working meetings in the Butler home.

- The amazing **staff of Ascension Press**, in particular **Matthew Pinto**, president, for his eager encouragement and bold approach to publishing within the New Evangelization, and **Steve Motyl**, Director of the Theology of the Body division, for his patience, humor, and brotherhood. Also to **Chris Cope**, Director of Marketing, **Mike Flickinger**, Managing Editor, and **Mike Fontecchio** and **Nick DeRose**, Graphic Designers, for their incredible dedication and professionalism.

CONTENTS

Note: Page numbers in this Leader's Guide match those of the Student Workbook. Blank pages, however, have been omitted. As such, leaders will notice a break in page sequence at certain points in the Leader's Guide.

It is Jesus in fact that you seek when you dream of happiness;

he is waiting for you when nothing else you find satisfies you;

he is the beauty to which you are so attracted; it is he who

provokes you with that thirst for fullness that will not let you

settle for compromise; it is he who urges you to shed the masks

of a false life; it is he who reads in your hearts your most

genuine choices, the choices that others try to stifle. It is Jesus

who stirs in you the desire to do something great with your

lives, the will to follow an ideal, the refusal to allow yourselves

to be ground down by mediocrity, the courage to commit

yourselves humbly and patiently to improving yourselves and

society, making the world more human and more fraternal.

– Blessed Pope John Paul II
August 19, 2000
World Youth Day (Rome)

LEADER'S INTRODUCTION

A Note to Leaders

We are excited and grateful that you have decided to lead your middle schoolers through this program! We live in a world of unprecedented opportunity and unprecedented challenge, especially for the generation of young people whom you serve. They are the first generation whose socialization has been largely digital. They communicate primarily through media detached from personal contact, such as texting or online social networks. They find practices such as silent reflection or extended lectures nearly unbearable, and they expect instant information and constant (and varied) stimulation.

They are a generation whose ability to reach into the world has far exceeded their ability to reflect and mature. Thus, they experience much confusion about love, identity, sexuality, and other fundamental aspects of human nature. While confusion about these issues is not new, a world of moral ambiguity is presented to them with unprecedented saturation.

Yet, in this darkness shines the Good News: Each of us is fearfully and wonderfully made, and God's truth about love, identity, and sexuality does not confuse but satisfies. The truth—wonderful and magnetic—has the power to free us from chaos. Young people, even middle schoolers, are hungry for this truth. In a perfect counterpoint to contemporary lies, we believe that Pope John Paul II presented this resonating truth in his Theology of the Body (TOB).

The Theology of the Body contains Blessed Pope John Paul II's teaching on the significance of humanity created male and female in the image and likeness of God. This teaching was originally delivered in 129 Wednesday audiences during his early papacy and represents his decades of reflection on the rich wisdom that Scripture, Tradition, and human experience provide on this topic. The TOB provides profound insight into the meaning of manhood and womanhood, thus shedding light on a host of moral issues. The Theology of the Body is available as a book, *Man and Woman He Created Them: A Theology of the Body*, translated by Michael Waldstein. This work contains all 129 Wednesday audiences, plus six undelivered audiences on the Song of Songs.

How does the TOB connect to middle schoolers? When looking out at a group of them, you see a thousand volts of energy and potential along with a vast range of experience, curiosity, and, in many cases, pain and disillusionment. This program ministers to their varied desires by answering life's two core questions, those which the Theology of the Body directly confronts: "Who am I?" and "How should I live?"

We have been amazed to see how the answers to these questions address nearly every difficulty faced by middle schoolers: body image, techno-socializing, dating, sin and reconciliation, healthy sharing of emotions, cyber bullying, weekend culture, and, of course, questions about sex and love. We will probe these throughout the program.

We know addressing these issues can be an intimidating task for parents, teachers, and youth ministers alike, so we have crafted this program keeping in mind the authentic teaching of John Paul II and the particular audience. In order for you to be well prepared and comfortable as a leader, we recommend that you review all eight chapters before you begin teaching. As you read, you will find that we have worked hard to respect the role of parents as primary educators and the varied levels of maturity that exist among this age group. For certain topics we have equipped you, the leader, with text and video to use at your discretion. We have also made extensive notes to help you to navigate sensitive issues.

To effectively form young people in chastity, we follow the lead of John Paul II and begin with our first parents' original experience, humanity's dilemma after sin, and the good news of our redemption in Christ. The *Theology of the Body for Teens: Middle School Edition* is much more than an abstinence education program; it also surpasses a traditional chastity program. It seeks to be an *identity* and *evangelization* program. The key to healthy sexuality is a relationship with Jesus Christ, because He is the key to knowing oneself. As the Second Vatican Council puts it, Christ came to reveal man to himself (see *Gaudium et Spes*, no. 22). By inviting middle schoolers into a deeper relationship with Him, we invite them into a healthy sense of self—and thus to a truly integrated sexuality.

Educators and youth leaders should be encouraged by these words of John Paul II:

> Sometimes when we look at the young, with the problems and weaknesses that characterize them in contemporary society, we tend to be pessimistic. The Jubilee of Young People, however, changed that, telling us that young people, whatever their possible ambiguities, have a profound longing for those genuine values which find their fullness in Christ. Is not Christ the secret of true freedom and profound joy of heart? Is not Christ the supreme friend and the teacher of all genuine friendship? If Christ is presented to young people as He really is, they experience Him as an answer that is convincing and they can accept His message,

even when it is demanding and bears the mark of the Cross. For this reason, in response to their enthusiasm, I did not hesitate to ask them to make a radical choice of faith and life and present them with a stupendous task: to become 'morning watchmen' (cf. Is 21:11-12) at the dawn of the new millennium. (*Novo Millennio Ineunte*, no. 9)

We pray that this program will serve you in helping your middle schoolers to make the same radical choice of faith and life that will surely change their lives.

Due to the ever-shifting, peer-pressure packed social landscape in which middle schoolers live daily, there is a pressing need for stability in order to live out their true identity and strength to pursue authentic love at all costs. May Blessed John Paul II intercede for you, that you would receive the graces of courage and steadfastness to help provide that stability. May we all learn to imitate Blessed John Paul II in both prayer and evangelization, that we may become holy and convincingly bring the message of life and love to the young "morning watchmen" of the new millennium.

Blessed John Paul II, pray for us!

– *Colin & Aimee MacIver, Jason Evert, and Brian Butler*
Divine Mercy Sunday
May 1, 2011

PROGRAM FEATURES

Objectives: Lays out the learning goals to keep in mind as you proceed through each chapter.

Notes and Nuggets: These comments are designed to help leaders best implement the program content and activities. They include further reading for leaders, considerations for difficult or sensitive topics, suggestions for lesson presentation, and instructions for program activities.

Tune In: Each chapter comes with several relevant song suggestions. Some work well with the opening prayer service, while others might just be fun songs to have playing during gathering or break times. All are great suggestions for youth to download and enjoy on their own.

Opening Prayer: This "call and response" styled prayer is repeated at the start of each chapter. It calls middle schoolers to remember throughout the program the greatness of God and His love for us, specifically as expressed through creating us male and female in His image and likeness. It concludes with an Our Father.

Icebreakers: These are fun, attention-grabbing options to creatively lead your group, through visual aids and physical activities, into the topic of the chapter.

Video: The companion DVD contains four content-specific features tailored for each chapter: 1. a dynamic introduction to set up the session; 2. questions and answers with authors and other experts to get the students thinking about the objectives; 3. man-on-the-street style candid interviews for fun reinforcement and discussion; 4. trivia questions for lively, interactive group review. We recommend using the first two features together near the beginning of the chapter and the other two together near the conclusion. You may, however, use them whenever they work best for your group and can even split them up further by going to "Scene Selection" on the DVD menu. Consider reading out loud to the group all of the on-screen graphics as they appear, including: session titles, questions and trivia.

Story Starter: A dramatic story that helps capture the attention of middle schoolers to draw them into the topic of the chapter.

Bridging the Gap: These few paragraphs link the preceding story to the lesson and prepare middle schoolers for the material they are about to cover.

To the Core: The main body of the teaching of the chapter.

In Your Faith: Interspersed throughout the body of the text, these breakout boxes isolate short catechetical themes relevant to the program. These items range from simple Scripture quotations or Catechism excerpts to a more detailed exploration of a particular doctrine.

If You Ask Me: These workbook exercises are intended to help middle schoolers engage and reflect upon and/or share an opinion or personal experience related to the chapter.

Mind Glue: Introduces memory devices to help middle schoolers remember key principles presented in the chapter.

Application: Provides activities that apply the chapter lesson to individual experiences. Some application activities can serve as formative assessments to help leaders check for comprehension and personal integration of the chapter topic, while other activities instruct middle schoolers how to construct tangible products that help them internalize and recall the lesson.

Work It Out: These assignments assess each student's learning. Assignments may be adapted to vary in difficulty and degree of involvement depending upon the needs of the group.

Closing Prayer with Scripture: Using a relevant Psalm as the connecting link, and concluding with a Glory Be, these simple prayers help close each chapter in a spirit of surrender to God.

Got It?: These workbook exercises are intended to be used as reviews and therefore are found near the end of each chapter. The purpose is to help the middle schoolers engage the text and improve reading comprehension.

Vocabulary: Each chapter concludes with a section of succinct definitions of the new terms introduced during the chapter. These words are bolded when they initially appear in a chapter, highlighting that this is a "key term" to understand.

Objectives:

At the end of this chapter, middle schoolers should be able to:

- Participate in an environment of trust and confidence in which they feel safe talking about important issues.
- Ask some basic, but critically important, questions about their own identities.
- Ask some basic, but critically important, questions about what it means to be a human person.
- Explore the basic nature of growing up, maturing, making decisions, and finding happiness.
- Learn what true freedom is and its purpose.
- Understand how Jesus' Incarnation reveals truth about their own lives.
- Discover the Theology of the Body as God's map given to help us find our way to true fulfillment as human persons.

Notes and Nuggets:

Effective conversations about deep issues require an environment in which your middle schoolers feel secure and affirmed. The program's personal nature calls for breaking the self-consciousness that keeps young people guarded and resistant. Chapter 1 focuses on creating an environment that supports effective teaching and discussion. Along with many reflective questions about middle schoolers' own experiences, this chapter provides several activities to establish a place where real connection can happen. At this point, you might want to space out icebreakers during the session. For a group that has already been together for a while, though, you might skip the name game and immediately go to one of the other activities. For a group that is just getting to know each other, the "Name Game" might be a good starter, while "Find Me Bingo" might serve as a better closing activity. Use your judgment to help your group bond from the very beginning.

Tune In:

Just Like You — Matt Maher, *Overflow*

This Is Your Life — Switchfoot, *Beautiful Letdown*

Here Am I? — Mercy Me, *Almost There*

Everything Glorious — David Crowder, *Everything Glorious*

Original — Kelly Pease, *self-titled*

Note: These songs are available online. Consider encouraging your students to find and download them.

Chapter One

Who Am I?

Discovering My True Identity

Notes and Nuggets:

This prayer should begin each lesson. A recurring prayer is a great tool for memory and connecting with God, and it also establishes tradition and stability.

Icebreakers

Name Game 2.0

Students sit in a circle and go around three times saying their names. (Tell them to pay close attention because there will be a quiz!) Each middle schooler then writes his/her name on three scraps of paper. Those papers are mixed into a hat. Each student picks three sheets of paper at random from the hat. Without talking, students must match the correct names to the correct people.

Find Me Bingo

Use Appendix #1 at the end of this Leader's Guide. This is a list of several random and interesting personality traits, likes and dislikes, etc. After distributing copies of the list, have your middle schoolers gather as many signatures as they can from others who match the described traits. Tell them that after seven minutes you will give prizes to the top three with the most signatures. (Be sure to have some simple prizes ready, such as candy or something funny/interesting.) This game establishes connections and common interests within the group. In order to complete the activity, middle schoolers must mingle with others they might not know well. Discussing the traits list after the game is a great opportunity to engage students in discussion about relevant interests and can help the leader discern which issues most concern the group.

Name and Detail Ball

On a volleyball or beach ball, use a permanent marker to write the following statements in different spots on the ball (do this before the activity to allow the ink to dry):

My favorite show is _____.

My favorite sports team is _____.

I brush my teeth with_____ toothpaste.

My middle name is _____.

If I could eat anywhere, I would eat at _____.

There is no such thing as _____.

On my next vacation I want to _____.

I never want to go back to _____.

I'm hoping to attend high school at

_____.

The best thing about my parents is

_____.

The hardest thing about being my age is

_____.

Have your middle schoolers toss the ball around the room while sitting in a circle. Whoever catches the ball must say his/her name and answer the statement on which his/her right index finger lands. Clarify that everyone should have a turn before there are any repeat throws to the same person.

 **VIDEO**

Play "Introduction" and "Big Questions" before Story Starter. Refer to Program Features on page ix for additional information and suggestions.

Leader: In the name of the Father and of the Son and of the Holy Spirit *(all make the Sign of the Cross).*

All respond: In the divine image, Lord, You created him; male and female You created them.

Reader 1: God, You made us good, both body and soul.

Response: In the divine image, Lord, You created him; male and female You created them.

Reader 2: God, You saw that it was not good for us to be alone, so You gave us one another for loving relationships.

Response: In the divine image, Lord, You created him; male and female You created them.

Reader 3: God, You are love, and You made us for love.

Response: In the divine image, Lord, You created him; male and female You created them.

Reader 4: God, You made us without anything to hide from You.

Response: In the divine image, Lord, You created him; male and female You created them.

Reader 5: God, You made us to be happy with You forever.

Response: In the divine image, Lord, You created him; male and female You created them.

Leader: Jesus, You taught us to address Your Father as You did, and so in the Holy Spirit we pray…

All: Our Father…

notes

)) STORY STARTER

You Can't Take It With You

At age eight, I decided to run away from home so I could drink orange juice whenever I wanted.

In my family, orange juice was a special treat reserved for birthdays and holidays. I had four younger siblings, and between us we could gulp down three gallons of juice a day, which got to be pretty expensive. So my mom had stopped buying orange juice as an everyday beverage. Our choices became limited to milk or water.

If I ran away, I would be able to buy my own juice and drink it all day long, if that's what I felt like doing. And maybe I would buy some Cocoa Puffs and

Notes and Nuggets:

Leaders, you are just getting warmed up. How you use the text in your particular setting is up to you. We have designed this program to be flexible and adaptable. You might want to read the story starter and use the text as notes which you present according to your own method. Alternatively, you might have your students take turns reading. Leaders with more time may want to divide each chapter's powerful concepts into several "bite-sized" lessons. With any approach, it is essential to keep the experience as interactive as possible. The student workbook offers a variety of quick-check questions, discussion starters, and other interactive components to keep your middle schoolers engaged.

Fruit Loops to replace Mom's standard menu of Cheerios and bananas. I couldn't wait to be on my own!

My friend Paul agreed to join me. Neither of us had any serious problems at home; we just wanted to be free. So we met up one morning after my mom had left the house to run errands. With plastic grocery bags in hand, we went through the house to gather up what we thought we would need for our journey and new life. Clothes, of course, but no church clothes, that was for sure. And medicine, but just the yummy grape chewable pills, not that nasty red syrup.

As we got ready to leave, Paul suggested bringing a few "survival" books to help us figure out which plants we could eat. We settled on the set of encyclopedias my grandfather had recently given my siblings and me. There were almost thirty volumes, but Paul and I put about two-thirds of the set into plastic bags and headed out the door.

At first, we were too excited to notice how heavy our bags were. We talked about where we would set up camp and how to start a fire with two sticks like they did on TV. Soon, the summer sun reached its full intensity. We started sweating bullets as we dragged the bags along the road. Man, they were heavy! Had they been this heavy when we left the house?

Neither of us wanted to admit it, but we realized that we had made a mistake. Did we really need all these books? Maybe we should go put some of them back. In fact, maybe running away wasn't worth the trouble. Things were pretty good at home. Our great plot ended with Paul going back home and me climbing into my bunk bed that night.

We experienced the desire to be free and make our own choices, but we obviously had no idea what to do with our freedom. We knew we needed something to guide us, but we packed all the wrong things and didn't even make it out of the neighborhood. We thought we had it all figured out, but we were really clueless about how to take care of ourselves in the wild. An entire set of encyclopedias was what we needed? Encyclopedias! Every pioneer who ever lived would have laughed to the point of tears.

It would still be years before either of us could set out on our own. First, we needed to know what a human person actually needs to survive and thrive.

– Aimee MacIver

IF YOU ASK ME ...

1. If I had to leave home tonight and could take only one thing with me, I would take_____.

2. When I was eight years old, my idea of freedom was _____.

In Your Faith

"What are humans that you are mindful of them, mere mortals that you care for them? Yet you have made them little less than a god, crowned them with glory and honor."

– Psalm 8:5-6

The Catechism of the Catholic Church *reminds us that we as human persons are the only creatures that God made just to love and be loved. Everything else God made— animals, plants, and even angels—was made to do a job or accomplish some task for Him or for humanity. This is why the* Catechism *reminds us that from our beginning we are made for eternal happiness with God (see CCC 1703).*

Notes and Nuggets:

At this point, present your students with a clear catechesis on the true nature of the human person. Remind them that we are the pinnacle of God's creation because we are made of the "stuff" of heaven (spirit) as well as the "stuff" of earth (body). This makes us earthly creatures with a heavenly homeland. God has given us, unlike the animals, free will to choose and guide us through life all the way back to be with Him in heaven. (For more on the uniqueness and greatness of the human person, see CCC 1730-1731 and 355-357.)

3. I think a human person needs _____ to survive.

4. I think a human person needs_____ to thrive.

BRIDGING THE GAP

You know those "Hello, my name is…" name tags?

If you walked into a room full of strangers and had to identify yourself without writing your actual name, what would your name tag say?

Would you describe your relationships? "I am Henry's granddaughter." "I am Sarah's brother." Would you give some details of your personality? "I am shy." "I am outgoing." You could explain what you do: "I am a soccer player." "I am a dancer." You could share your likes: "I like pizza." "I like riding horses." Or maybe you would just state the obvious: "I am a boy." "I am a girl."

All of these things would certainly describe parts of your identity. Even if your likes or hobbies changed, you would still exist, so really, deep down, the question remains: Who are you as a human person?

You actually began trying to define your identity when you were a toddler. You learned how many years "old" you were and proudly counted out three fingers to anyone who would listen. You learned how to spell your name and then wrote it on everything. You and your friends spent hours pretending to be different

characters: firefighters, ballerinas, football stars, chefs, veterinarians. Remember as a little kid playing house or "army" inside a homemade fort?

But why did you, like most kids, play games about being someone older? You don't see first graders running around the playground at recess saying, "Let's pretend to be first graders at recess." Even at an early age, we are motivated to develop into more than what we are now.

IF YOU ASK ME …

1. Three relationships that helped make me who I am today:

_____

_____

_____

2. What I think makes humans different from animals is:

_____

_____

In Your Faith

When it comes to the big question of what it means to be human, our Catholic faith gives us some profound answers. The first section of the Catechism of the Catholic Church *tells us that human beings are the only creatures that God made for their own sakes. This means that God made us just because He loves us. He wasn't lonely or bored. He doesn't need us. He just loves and wants to share His life with us. That's really good news!*
(see CCC 1 & 355)

Notes and Nuggets:

The following paragraphs begin to examine some specific examples of the transition experienced by middle schoolers. Remind your group that it is normal to experience confusion at their age. For example, girls may find themselves crying "for no reason," while boys may find themselves feeling angry without knowing why. Middle schoolers are experiencing major biological changes and may start to compare themselves to each other. They may also feel more tension in their relationships with their parents. During these changes, it is encouraging to remember that God created everyone good. As we grow each day, He wants us to accept ourselves as He does. We are unique, unrepeatable, irreplaceable gifts to the world—male and female created in His image and likeness. Nothing can change that truth.

The next three chapters will expand upon who we are as human persons, but now is also a good time to survey what preconceived ideas your students bring into the program, as well as to affirm what they already know.

You could pose the question "What makes us human?" or "What are some things that all human beings have in common?" If you have time for tangential discussion, you could conduct a thought experiment: "If you had to explain human beings to an alien who had never met one, how would you do it?" Let your middle schoolers brainstorm and have volunteers write their ideas on the board, or break them into small groups and have them make lists on poster-board. This is a good strategy to begin steering their personal experiences toward what John Paul II calls an "adequate anthropology."

If the following points do not surface, you may want to make them as a sort of final word: Distinctly human capacities are intellect, free will, and the ability to love.

TO THE CORE

From the moment we are born, **human persons** have a deep desire to grow up, be independent, and find happiness. In many ways, this is a good thing, because otherwise we would never make any progress. Can you imagine what the world would be like if everyone refused to be potty trained?

At this point in your life, you are probably starting to feel the urge to have more freedom, to make more of your own choices, to experience life more like an adult. Sometimes you might feel restless or annoyed when parents or teachers tell you what to do, simply because you want to do your own thing, not theirs. This desire is natural and necessary to help you discover who you are and who you want to become.

Having independence and finding happiness become more complicated as we grow up. You want to make your own choices, but sometimes you don't know what to choose. You want to find happiness, but sometimes you are not sure where to look for it. As a kid, choices were pretty simple: Should you choose chocolate or vanilla ice cream? Now your decisions matter more: If you speak up in class, will you look stupid? Should you hang out with your friends and risk failing tomorrow's test, or should you study diligently but miss the fun?

Happiness was also easier to pinpoint in childhood. Some candy and new toys pretty much did it. You spent all day playing, and your biggest responsibility was washing your hands before dinner. Now you spend all day at school, and you are expected to make good grades, practice hard, complete your chores, and maybe even watch your younger siblings.

So it's a sort of trade-off. The more freedom you have, the more your happiness depends on your own choices.

Even your friendships change as you grow up. In kindergarten, your friends didn't care about your clothes or if you had a boyfriend or girlfriend. If you wanted to impress them, you jumped on your bed or blew bubbles in your milk. Boys hung out with other boys and thought girls were good for nothing but chasing around the playground. Girls cared for their dolls and played dress-up. The two groups were more often separated than together.

Now, it's different. Your group of friends is changing. You may find out you don't share much in common anymore with old friends from elementary school. You may want to spend more time with the opposite gender. You may feel more concerned with your looks and more confused about how to be accepted. The changes can be pretty overwhelming. What should you wear? What should you say? Will people like you?

This is exactly when knowing who you really are as a human person matters most.

Notes and Nuggets:

This chapter's application is in an expanded "If You Ask Me..." in the student workbook. Students should silently fill in the "If You Ask Me..." and then discuss how their desires changed as they got older. Be sure to tell them that God wants to fulfill their truest desires and that their purest longings were actually placed in their hearts by God Himself. Ultimately, we all seek love. If this reality does not naturally surface in their answers, you can pose the following question to start a group discussion: "Do you think it is fair to say that what we are all really after is love?"

IF YOU ASK ME ...

1. When I was five, all I wanted was _____.

2. When I was six, I wanted to be a _____ when I grew up.

3. When I was seven, I would have watched _____ all day if my mom let me.

4. When I was eight, my favorite subject in school was _____.

5. When I was nine, I was afraid of _____, but not now.

6. Right now, I want _____ more than anything.

7. When I'm sixteen, I hope I can _____.

8. When I get to college, I'm going to _____.

9. When I'm old, I hope I'll be able to say that I _____.

10. My biggest goal is to be a _____ person.

11. In the end, I think all anyone really wants is _____.

You can't make such decisions until you know who you are. It is like trying to find a place you have never been to before without having a map or a GPS. Imagine you want to visit the beach. To get there, you hop in the car, back out of your driveway, and start turning down random roads, hoping one will take you to the ocean. If you tried to travel this way, most of your turns would be dead ends; they would lead you anywhere but where you wanted to go. You would be no closer to your goal, and maybe even farther away than when you started. And you would have lost precious time that you could have been spending in the sand.

IF YOU ASK ME ...

Even though _____ is invisible, I know it is real because _____. (Give an example of something that you are sure is real even though it is invisible. Then explain how you can be sure of this.) _____

Looking for the Beach

Unfortunately, just when you really need examples of what it means to be a free, happy person, it is harder than ever to find them. What do you see teenagers doing on TV and in movies? They are drinking alcohol at parties. They are getting into really intense dating relationships. They are often doing pretty much what they want without rules. And they usually seem cool and

Notes and Nuggets:

"Cookie Quest"

The following activity is an optional closing to the chapter. It may not be appropriate for every setting, but it can help drive home the image of a map and also provide another bonding opportunity. Bonding, fun, trust, and an overall positive rapport are important for laying the groundwork of this program.

Before your group meets, hide cookies throughout the room and/or building. There should be at least one cookie for each student. Cookies should be grouped and labeled according to groups of three. Organize your middle schoolers into groups of three and give each group a map to their cookies. The map should require some decoding. See the example directions below. You, of course, will make directions that correspond to your particular situation. If possible, it might be more fun to hide cookies outside of your room. Instruct each group to find the cookies and then return. You will need adult chaperones to monitor the groups.

This activity is meant to be lighthearted. Once your middle schoolers have returned and are eating their cookies, you can explain that the Theology of the Body is like the map to the cookies. We need to follow God's map in order to get to the "really good stuff" that He has prepared for us.

Group 1:

Start on the X.

Go over to the blue chair in the back of the classroom and take four steps to the right.

Back up two steps.

Look down.

Enjoy!

Group 2:

Start on the X.

Go out the front door into the hallway and take a right.

Walk exactly halfway down the hallway and take a right.

Look down.

Enjoy!

sophisticated. According to these images, freedom means doing whatever you want; happiness is having fun and avoiding complications.

In real life, some adults may not give very good examples either. Many adults seem to live by the idea that one's identity comes from one's career. Happiness means you have a nice house and a new car every three years. Yet you may have noticed that this way of life doesn't really guarantee anything at all. How many adults have you seen who do nothing but work, complain, and remain frustrated? You may even have seen supposedly "successful" adults who treat each other unkindly, or who seem incapable of good relationships.

No wonder young people today seem so confused about who they are, what will give them true happiness, and what maturity means. Some guys might think they are supposed to hook up with as many girls as they can to prove they are men. Some girls might think they have to show off their bodies or flirt all the time to attract a boyfriend.

The world is not all bad, but it certainly is confused about what makes a person matter—and it is even more confused about what makes a person happy. It is sometimes easy to get the idea that you are worth nothing more than how good you look, how well you perform, and how much you own.

But God loved us too much to leave us confused! At the **Incarnation**, God the Son actually became one of us and opened a way for us to end up even better off than Adam and Eve started. And God did not stop helping humanity after the time of Jesus. He gives us exactly what we need for the time we live in.

One of God's main ways of helping humanity is to inspire holy men and women with wisdom that they can share with others. We know these people as the saints. God inspired Blessed John Paul II, although he is not yet a canonized **saint**, with answers to those questions you have about identity and happiness. John Paul II was a man who truly loved youth. He understood how difficult it can be to find the truth when TV, movies, music, magazines, and society surround you with mistaken ideas. So John Paul II spoke about the true meaning of who you are in a collection of talks called the **Theology of the Body**. The Theology of the Body asks and answers two big questions: *Who am I? How should I live?* This teaching is like a map that reveals how our visible bodies can express the truth about our invisible souls. It reveals many things about our relationships with God and others, such as:

- You have the freedom to choose how you will live your life.

- You have been created for loving relationships with God and others.

- These truths about our own relationships help us understand the relationship of the Holy Trinity: the One God is Three Persons—the Father, the Son, and the Holy Spirit—who love each other eternally.

In Your Faith

Jesus not only gave us a map; He is also the guide! Check out what He says in John 14:6: "I am the way, the truth, and the life."

"And the Word became flesh and made his dwelling among us." – John 1:14

"The Word became flesh" refers to the Incarnation, when God the Son assumed a human nature in order to accomplish our salvation in it (CCC 461). God became one of us to save us!

VIDEO

Play "Man on the Street" and "Trivia" before Work it Out.

Notes and Nuggets:

The "Work It Out" section provides options for processing and assessment. In this first chapter the activities are geared toward helping students share their thoughts and interests. One suggestion is to allow time during the next several sessions for one or two young people to share their self-portrait.

Notes and Nuggets:

If you assign "Work It Out – Getting to Know Me" and decide to have your middle schoolers present their projects, explain that the projects will not be presented without you previewing them first. This will prevent potential awkwardness during sharing, and it will ensure that the experience uplifts the whole group's dynamic.

If you assign "Media Mash Up," be prepared to play the CDs or DVDs to the class or individual group.

This workbook will help you to learn more about what God inspired this great pope to share with us.

So there is hope—a lot of hope! You can start high school confident and happy about who you are and what kind of person you will become. You can have good relationships with your friends and with those of the opposite gender. God offers you a destination better than anything like popularity, money, or power could offer. And, more importantly, God offers you a map; even more importantly than that, He gave us Jesus to be our guide along the way.

Are you ready to go?

IF YOU ASK ME ...

I think _____ is a good role model.

WORK IT OUT

A. Getting to Know Me

Create a symbolic collage or self-portrait (drawn by you or from an image search) to represent your uniqueness. Put the images together in a Power Point presentation, a collage, or some other artistic piece. Include some of the following elements:

- a personality trait that makes people laugh
- a personality trait your friends value most about you
- a secret talent or weird ability
- something good you have done for someone else
- a favorite "something" (but be original—no people, songs, movies, foods, animals, or colors!)
- three blessings God has given you
- quotations from three different family members, friends, and teachers describing something they love, appreciate, or admire about you. (Don't quote the same person twice!)

B. Media Mash Up

Create a collection of songs (on CD) or video clips (on DVD) that you believe show the challenging process of growing up. Explain your choices in a brief written paragraph or present your collection to the group or class.

Closing Prayer

Let us thank God for the Good News we have heard in this chapter as we pray:

The LORD is my shepherd; I shall not want.
He guides me in right paths for His name's sake.
Even though I walk in the dark valley I fear no evil.

You are at my side with Your rod and Your staff that give me courage.

Glory be to the Father and to the Son and to the Holy Spirit. As it was in the beginning, is now, and ever shall be, world without end. Amen.

– From Psalm 23

Got It?

1. saints

2. Theology of the Body

3. happiness

Notes and Nuggets:

Each chapter concludes with a vocabulary section which contains definitions to key terms set off in bold text throughout each chapter. In a school setting, a leader might encourage students to make flashcards and/or conduct a quiz or vocabulary quiz game. This sort of check up, whether formal or informal, can help to ensure comprehension and retention of the new words used in each chapter.

GOT IT?

1. Holy men and women inspired by God to share their wisdom with others are called _____.

2. Pope John Paul II spoke about the true meaning of who you are in a collection of talks called the _____.

3. The more freedom you have, the more your _____ depends on your own choices.

VŌ·CAB′·U·LAR′·Ȳ

HUMAN PERSON:

God created us with both a body and a soul. We are the only creatures God made in His image and likeness, made to love and be loved. All other earthly creatures were made for our benefit. Every human person is unique and unrepeatable. This fact flows from being created in God's image and likeness, which is uniquely true about humans.

INCARNATION:

The Incarnation refers to the reality that Jesus, who is fully God, became man. God the Son became man so He could die and rise, saving humanity from the destruction caused by sin so that we can really become sons and daughters of God, possessing divine life.

SAINT:

A saint is someone who has lived a holy life, practiced virtue to a heroic degree, and chosen to love God above all things. Saints come from around the world and from different backgrounds. Some are priests and nuns, others are married, and some are even children. The Catholic Church canonizes, or gives the title of saint, to those holy men and women to give us examples of how we should live too. We are all called to become saints.

THEOLOGY OF THE BODY:

On Wednesdays from 1979 to 1984, Pope John Paul II gave talks about how the body reveals that human persons are created in the image of God, as male and female, with freedom for loving relationships. The Theology of the Body asks and answers two big questions: *Who am I? How should I live?*

Objectives:

At the end of this chapter middle schoolers should be able to:

- Reflect on the experience of sin.
- Reflect on the experience of sin as a cheap substitute for authentic good.
- Explore how God's original plan for us was a pure and perfect relationship.
- Understand original sin as a lost inheritance.
- Anticipate the hope that Jesus brings us to heal the brokenness and divisions we experience.

Notes and Nuggets:

This program aims to introduce the Theology of the Body in an accessible way to middle school students' growth now, as well as for deeper exploration in high school and beyond. Chapter 2 challenges middle schoolers to consider how their experiences of brokenness and sin contrast with humanity's origins when, as Jesus says, "it was not so." Connecting your young people with their personal experiences of desire, sin, hope, and even confusion shows how these experiences echo our first parents' original state as well as their sin. This program adapts the content of John Paul II's audiences to provide middle schoolers with a deeper vision of what it means to be a human person created in God's image and likeness, wounded by sin, and restored by grace.

Tune In:

Amazing Grace/My Chains are Gone — Chris Tomlin, *See the Morning*

Ooh-Ahh — Grits, *The Art of Translation*

Gone — Switchfoot, *Beautiful Letdown*

I'm Not Alright — Sanctus Real, *The Face of Love*

Note: These songs are available online. Consider encouraging your students to find and download them.

Chapter
Two

Our Story
God's Plan, Human Sin, Jesus' Love

Opening Prayer:

Lead an opening prayer service. You can close this prayer with something along the lines of "Lord, help us, through this chapter, to understand better the story of our beginning, created in your love. Help us to see clearly our need for you and to recognize your plan to save us. Amen."

Icebreakers

Taste Test

Bring in samples of both brand-name and generic versions of a few foods. For the sake of the activity, your generic versions should be particularly poor knockoffs, e.g., imitation Oreos or faux Coca-Cola. Blindfold your students and instruct them to taste-test both the brand-name and the generic samples. Despite approximations in appearances and flavor, most will immediately taste the inferior quality of the imitations. This activity serves as an engaging introduction to the characteristic of sin as a cheap imitation of the true good.

Notes and Nuggets:

After conducting the icebreaker, explain how sin is only a pale imitation of the real good we seek. God wants to give us the real thing, while the devil only wants to lure us in with a counterfeit. Sin is tempting because it is desirable, but it never really "hits the spot." Only the real thing (God's love) can do that.

VIDEO

Play "Introduction" and "Big Questions" before Story Starter.

Opening Prayer

Leader: In the name of the Father and of the Son and of the Holy Spirit *(all make the Sign of the Cross).*

All respond: In the divine image, Lord, You created him; male and female You created them.

Reader 1: God, You made us good, both body and soul.

Response: In the divine image, Lord, You created him; male and female You created them.

Reader 2: God, You saw that it was not good for us to be alone, so You gave us one another for loving relationships.

Response: In the divine image, Lord, You created him; male and female You created them.

Reader 3: God, You are love, and You made us for love.

Response: In the divine image, Lord, You created him; male and female You created them.

Reader 4: God, You made us without anything to hide from You.

Response: In the divine image, Lord, You created him; male and female You created them.

Reader 5: God, You made us to be happy with You forever.

Response: In the divine image, Lord, You created him; male and female You created them.

Leader: Jesus, You taught us to address Your Father as You did, and so in the Holy Spirit we pray...

All: Our Father...

notes

He-Man in the Garden of Eden

When I was five, my mom took me shopping to buy a present for my friend Matthew's birthday. His big party was the next day, and I had been thinking about it all week. Like all five-year-olds, I loved birthday parties: games, friends, excitement, and—let's just be honest—that cake-and-ice-cream sugar high! I knew Matthew's party would be one to remember.

We went to Ray Willis Toy Store to buy the gift. Ray Willis wasn't a chain store with a tiny toy department hidden behind endless aisles of groceries and other boring adult stuff. Ray Willis was 100 percent toys and games, every kid's fantasy. Wall to wall, from aisle to aisle, it was packed with

games, action figures, trucks, bikes, even candy. Ray Willis Toy Store was so awesome that my heart beat faster just thinking about the paradise inside.

As I walked down an aisle, something caught my eye. Among the hundreds of other toys, this one grabbed my attention: a sword. But not just any sword. This sword talked, had working lights, was bright and shiny, and looked exactly like the sword He-Man used to defeat evil villains on TV. He-Man was my favorite action superhero when I was a kid, and this sword mesmerized me. I was awestruck.

"Mom!" I yelled in an awkwardly loud voice. "He-Man sword! He-Man sword! I need it! It's what I've always wanted!"

As mothers sometimes must, she burst my bubble. "Honey, remember why we're here. Tomorrow is Matthew's birthday and we're here to shop for him. You can get a toy for yourself some other day."

Like a typical five-year-old, I persisted: "But Mom! It's THE HE-MAN SWORD. I NEED IT!" And then I threw an outrageous tantrum right there in the middle of the store.

As I flailed and screamed on the floor, my mom kept her cool and made the following deal with me: "Okay. You can have the sword. But I am going to give you a choice. If you get the sword, you can't go to the party because you won't have a gift. And you have to call Matthew and tell him why you can't come."

In my child's mind, I thought, *she's bluffing*. Without hesitation I snatched the sword from the shelf, clutched it tightly to my chest, and hustled to the cash register to seal the deal. Mine, all mine! My He-Man sword! My precious He-Man sword!

My mom kept her word. She looked disappointed but paid the cashier. Without saying anything, she walked with me back to the car. I gripped the sword and fantasized about all the cool stuff I could do now that I possessed it! But then, as my mom buckled me in, something deep inside my young self lit up. I suddenly worried that maybe she had not been bluffing. "Uh, Mom?" I gulped.

"Yes?"

"Do I really have to skip the party?"

She answered firmly, "Yep. That's what you chose."

The words hit me hard. I was afraid to ask the next question: "Do I really have to call Matthew?"

"Yes. That was the deal."

Notes and Nuggets:

We recommend taking some time for sharing here. You may also find it helpful to share your own answers. These sorts of questions can be disarming and helpful in setting the stage for some of the deeper discussion in this chapter.

And then the crying started: hot tears, followed by runny snot, followed by loud sobbing. "I don't want it anymore! I want to go to Matthew's party! I want to take the sword back!"

But my choice had been made. My mom stuck to her guns. She had given me a choice: to be a giver or a taker. She warned me what would happen if I made the wrong choice—I would be alone and possibly hurt my friend's feelings.

The afternoon I called Matthew to tell him I had chosen a plastic sword over him is one I will never forget. A week later, I was alone in the backyard playing with the sword when it broke. In the end, I had nothing to show for my selfish choice.

– Colin MacIver

IF YOU ASK ME ...

1. The toughest lesson I learned from my parents was when

   _____.

2. The best birthday or holiday party I ever went to was _____.

3. One time I chose _____ when I should have chosen

   _____.

BRIDGING THE  GAP

All of the questions we asked about identity and happiness in Chapter 1 can be traced back to one moment in human history: the first sin. Why? Think about what makes sense. God is perfect and everything He does is perfect. If God never makes mistakes, then it is impossible that He would have created the first human persons in a way that made them incapable of living His plan of happiness for them. Before the first sin, the first humans needed to discover who they were, but it was not a struggle. They didn't experience the confusion we experience now. They didn't struggle with questions the same way we do, because their minds were truly free from the confusing tug of sin. They knew who they were and what their purpose was. They were free.

But if the first human persons were created without sin, how did the disaster of sin happen?

Well, some things never change. Within every temptation to sin is a dangerous scam. The benefit we think we see in sin is a trick designed to lead us into destruction. Just as the He-Man sword seemed so desirable that it justified selfishness, so does sin.

Notes and Nuggets:

Without creating a "group confession," engage your students for a few moments in a brief discussion about the results of selfishness in their lives or in the lives of others. Rather than merely focusing on the choices made, invite them to share a few words about the negative consequences and feelings they and others experienced as a result of their selfishness. Help them see the common thread that is sure to surface: regret, frustration, guilt, sadness, anger, confusion, stress, loneliness, fear, etc. You can then point out how none of these things come from being generous and loving. Instead, generous choices of love—even when they call for sacrifice—always bring things like confidence, freedom, joy, peace, and hope.

Notes and Nuggets:

Whenever John Paul II uses the term "in the beginning," he is referring not merely to the book of Genesis, but specifically to the time before sin. This era—of which we all have a heritage in our hearts—is what he calls the "original" experiences of man and woman. The three main original experiences he focuses upon are original solitude, original unity, and original nakedness. (For more on these, see TOB 1 through TOB 19.)

If you've ever dealt with email spam, you have a good idea of how sin tricks us. We are attracted by the promises of pleasure and fun and freedom. But when we pursue it, spam infects us and slows down the functions the computer was made for. Clicking on a link in just one spam email triggers a flood of even more spam that is almost impossible to remove. Without correction, spam eventually destroys the hard drive altogether.

When we sin, we are attracted by the false promises of pleasure and freedom. We choose a false good instead of trusting that following God's laws will lead us to what is really good. We have chosen the sword instead of the party, but now we're alone in the backyard with a broken toy instead of enjoying cake with friends. We are never satisfied when we focus only on ourselves. Have you ever met someone who was both selfish and really happy?

If we really examine our human experience, we see that not only are the toys broken, but so are we. We need serious repairs. Think about the ways we show our brokenness. Even if we know sin will hurt us, we keep choosing sin because it seems good in the moment. Even when we know sin will hurt others, we convince ourselves that it's okay.

Have you ever had a moment when you realized how bad and selfish some of your choices have been? Sometimes, we have moments of really wanting to take back our sins and do good. We experience regret but still find ourselves sinning over and over again. We find it so hard to stop on our own.

So what can we do about it?

We can look to God, who is the exact opposite of self-centered sin: God is love. Instead of thinking only of Himself, He never stops thinking about you. Every law God ever gave was to help you get to His party and enjoy that wonderful, sugar-soaked cake. Then sin distracts us, and we begin to think that we know better than God who made us. But when we follow our own way instead of God's, the only place we end up is alone.

IF YOU ASK ME ...

God is_____. (Write the first word that comes to your mind.)

In Your Faith

"God created man in His image; in the divine image He created him; male and female He created them."

– Genesis 1:27

The Catechism *helps us understand what this verse means. You and every person you know are made in God's image and so reflect some aspect of God to the world. Yet human persons reflect God most clearly in our relationships with one another, especially when we form loving relationships with our friends and families (see CCC 1702).*

"When God, in the beginning, created man, he made him subject to his own free choice ... Before man are life and death, whichever he chooses shall be given him." – Sirach 15:14, 17

TO THE CORE

How did things get like this? Surely God did not make us for this mess!

We need to go back to Eden—**to the beginning**—to a story many of us heard as children. God did not need anything or anyone else. God is love, first and foremost because the Father, Son, and Holy Spirit—three truly

Notes and Nuggets:

In this chapter, we will begin to break open the story in which we all have a place. A big part of John Paul II's "adequate anthropology" is realizing that every human person—as a member of humanity—has an amazing story, even if we don't realize it at first. This is why Blessed John Paul II went to great lengths to show that we all have a "distant echo" (TOB 19:2) of what he calls "original innocence"—peace of life before the Fall, which was void of sin and its effects. This purity of our origin is part of the story that we so often miss, the part where man knew, through experience, the greatness of God's gift as an embodied person created in God's image.

Throughout this program, remind your middle schoolers that their own personal story is a reflection of their identity within the pool of salvation history. The common wisdom is true: to understand yourself, you must know where you have come from, where you are now, and where you are going. The story of where we have come from is what John Paul II called "Original Man," that is, humanity in its state of original innocence prior to the Fall as seen in Genesis.

The story of where we are now is what John Paul II called "Historical Man," which is the era from the fall of Adam until the end of the world. Right in the center of this history is the Incarnation—the life, death, and resurrection of Christ. While it is easy to lose hope when looking at the world around us today, we must remember that Christ is the center of our story and, therefore, the center of our story is full of hope! And toward what does our hope point? Heaven.

The story of where we are going is about our destiny—life forever with God in heaven—which John Paul II called "Eschatological Man." These three parts—our origin, history, and destiny—comprise the great story in which we all play a part. Forgetting any part of the story is to miss a key to who we really are: beloved sons and daughters of God, created in grace and saved in hope as we look to our life with God in eternity. Remind your middle schoolers that the story of their lives is truly epic—bigger than any blockbuster movie!

distinct Divine Persons—have loved each other eternally. God is complete in Himself. Yet God's love is so great that He wanted to share it. He created man and woman **in His image and likeness**. This meant that when Adam and Eve loved one another, they would be like a model of the Trinity's love. God gave Adam and Eve all good things, including a perfect paradise where they could live without suffering, or any problems in their relationship. They could not have asked for—or even imagined—anything better than what God gave them freely.

Imagine the blessing this life was in the beginning! No insecurity. No drama. No family problems, no homework, and no wondering whether or not you fit in. All they needed to do was continue trusting God to provide.

Because God's only desire was for them to love Him and each other, He gave Adam and Eve **free will**, which is the ability to choose. God gave Adam and Eve free will because love is not possible otherwise. True love is not possible without choice because you cannot force someone to love you, and nobody can force you to love him or her. Love is not love at all unless it is freely given.

You have probably experienced this reality in your own life with things less significant than relationships. Maybe you have been encouraged (or even forced) to try a hobby or eat a food that you just didn't like. No matter how much someone encouraged or pushed you, your heart just wasn't in it. If it is impossible to force people to love hobbies or food, how could it be possible to force the most important love of all—human love for another and for God?

Free will makes love possible, but the ability to choose what is right goes together with the ability to choose what is wrong. God knew that Satan, the enemy of love, would try to take advantage of Adam and Eve's free will and trick them into choosing wrong. But God loved Adam and Eve so much that He prepared them to face that temptation. He was like a parent telling a child, "If you touch that hot stove, you'll burn your hand!" God told His children what would happen if they used their free will to choose wrong— they would die! (Genesis 2:17)

Sure enough, Satan soon told Adam and Eve a very tempting lie. He said God was like a dictator trying to repress them so they wouldn't become as powerful as He. Despite the overwhelming evidence that God loved them, Adam and Eve chose wrong. They disobeyed God. And just as God had warned, death followed sin.

Death came to four different relationships that had been perfect before sin.

First, Adam and Eve's relationship with the physical part of their world was damaged. All kinds of bodily suffering began: injury, defects, disease.

In Your Faith

"For us there is one God, the Father, from whom all things are and for whom we exist, and one Lord, Jesus Christ, through whom all things are and through whom we exist." –1 Corinthians 8:6

Notes and Nuggets:

We will now describe how original sin operates. For a vivid visual aid that illustrates the "spread" of sin, hold up a large, clear container filled with clean water. Point out the water's purity and suitability for drinking. As you explain how one sin affected the collective purity of the human race, squeeze one drop of liquid red food coloring into the water. Do not stir or shake the container; the red dye will begin to spread slowly until the water becomes totally red. You can explain the illustration: one sin damaged the entire goodness of creation.

Instead of always having everything they needed for their bodies, they would now have to struggle constantly to maintain food and shelter. Even now, we experience this consequence in our own lives. We get sick, we get hurt, and, someday, all of us will die.

Second, another type of death is a spiritual death. Death, by definition, is the ultimate separation of the body from the soul. This is what Adam and Eve experienced individually. Before the Fall, Adam's bodily actions always followed his pure soul. The same went for Eve; her actions followed her pure heart. This is holiness. But when they went against the law God had placed in their heart and sinned with their bodies, they experienced a split within themselves, a sort of death.

Third, Adam and Eve's perfect relationship with each other died. Instead of perfectly loving and accepting each other, they began to experience tension and misunderstanding. They covered their bodies because sin made them feel insecure. Don't we still deal with the same issues? We fight with family members; we feel insecure about our looks; we worry whether or not we are loved.

Fourth, and worst of all, their perfect relationship with God died. Instead of being in total union with Him, they were cut off from God, like a kite being cut off its string. God did not stop loving Adam and Eve, but they chose to reject His love, thinking they would find something better. Of course, because God had made them, He knew what was really best for them. Adam and Eve soon saw that nothing better than God's love exists, because all good things come from His love.

After being cut off from the source of love itself, Adam and Eve's ability to love suffered major injury. Imagine a car having its engine yanked out from under its hood. You wouldn't get very far in that car, would you? In a similar way, we won't get very far in our relationships without the "engine" of God's love.

Original Sin

Adam and Eve's sin was passed on to the whole human race. We call this **original sin**. Original sin is something like a lost inheritance. Adam and Eve had been given a perfect world, but their sin wasted this treasure like a stack of money being set on fire. Money that has been burned is not misplaced or saved for later; it is simply gone. In the same way, original sin spent humanity's inheritance of holiness.

God designed human nature to desire holiness and choose good easily. With our spiritual inheritance gone, we now find it really difficult to overcome sin. It's like not having enough money. When you have easy access to lots of money, you can purchase what you need without a second thought. Without

In Your Faith

When it comes to defining a human person, our faith teaches us that we are each created in the image and likeness of God. So to be human is a call to be like God, but how? The Catechism says that when we are together in love, we are like the Trinity (see CCC 1702). God is not a lonely old guy with a beard. God is three Persons in a perfect relationship. We are made for relationship, too, and when we are together, we reflect God!

APPLICATION

Divide the class into two teams.

Using a chalkboard or dry-erase board, create a simple game board with ten spaces from the start to the finish. The first team to reach the end wins the game.

You will be making several statements, some true and others false. After each statement is made, have your teams discuss whether or not the statement is a scam. A representative of the team will bring a paper verdict to the front of the classroom. If the team's verdict is correct, they will move forward one space closer to the finish. If not, they will stay on the same space.

This is a glorified true/false quiz, with you playing the role of devil's advocate. Demonstrate to your group that it takes only a little lie to infect an entire statement. In fact, good scams work because they are partially true. In the same way, sin tempts us with a partial truth infected with lies and disobedience.

Read the following statements for the game:

- God told Adam and Eve that the fruit was evil. *(False. He simply told them not to eat it. See Genesis 2:17.)*

- Adam was created out of Eve's rib. (*False. Eve was created from Adam's rib. See Genesis 2:22-23.*)

- Adam and Eve were created naked and without shame. *(True. See Genesis 2:25.)*

- The first command God gave Adam and Eve was not to eat the fruit. *(False. His first order was to be fruitful and multiply. See Genesis 1:28.)*

- God made clothes for Adam and Eve after they discovered they were naked. *(True. See Genesis 3:21.)*

- The river that flowed out of Eden split to become two rivers. *(False. It split to become four rivers. See Genesis 2:10.)*

- It was good for the man to be alone. *(False. It was not good for the man to be alone. See Genesis 2:18.)*

- God said that the serpent would crawl on his belly and eat dirt! *(True. See Genesis 3:14.)*

- God said that Adam would now have to sweat to earn his bread. *(True. See Genesis 3:19.)*

- God put an angel with a fiery sword to guard the way to the tree of knowledge. *(False. The angel guarded the tree of life. See Genesis 3:24.)*

Sin destroys relationships. Here is an easy way to remember the four relationships that original sin destroyed:

1. Adam and Eve's relationship with the physical world—NATURE

2. Adam's body and soul relationship; Eve's body and soul relationship—SELF

3. Adam and Eve's relationship with each other—OTHERS

4. Adam and Eve's relationship with God—GOD

enough money, though, it's a struggle to buy anything, because you just don't have the cash.

Original sin triggered the cycle of broken relationships and selfishness that we all recognize. After Adam and Eve, their son Cain killed his brother, Abel, simply because Cain was jealous. Just like his parents, Cain had been warned by God that choosing wrong would cause a domino effect of misery. He knew his wrong choice would hurt himself and others. He did it anyway.

Sound familiar?

Cravings of the Heart

Have you ever had a craving for a very specific food, like vanilla ice cream, but you didn't have any ice cream in the freezer? Trying to find a substitute for what you really want, you open the fridge and stand there with the door open until your mom yells at you to stop air-conditioning the whole house. Maybe yogurt will do. It's creamy and sweet like ice cream, right? One bite, though, and it's obvious that Yoplait ain't no Ben and Jerry's. You still want ice cream, now more than ever! And the more you try to substitute for what you really crave, the more intense the craving gets.

But if you do find a pint of Ben and Jerry's tucked in the back of the freezer, what happens? Heaven! You scoop a big bowl, grab a spoon, and start slurping it down before you even get back to the couch. Your craving is satisfied; that annoying urge lightens up and you feel … content.

More important than a craving for temporary pleasure, our hearts have even more powerful cravings for happiness, purpose, and love. You can probably guess that when God made Adam and Eve, these cravings were totally satisfied by their closeness to God and to each other. Sadly, when sin cut off humanity from God's love, our heart's deepest desires remained, but we lost sight of how to satisfy them.

So what do craving hearts do? They try to find substitutes for what they really want. They try one thing after another, but because nothing really hits the spot, the cycle just continues. The world offers all kinds of substitutes. Just consider some commercials you've seen. Almost all of them try to convince us that if we buy the product, we will be happy and successful.

But if that were true, then we would need to buy the product only once and we would be happy for the rest of our lives. Is that reality? Has a product ever made anyone say, "That's all I need until I die. Don't give me anything else. I don't want anything more because this thing is enough to keep me happy for the next sixty years."

We can just walk into any shopping mall to see the craziness of the idea that stuff can make and keep our heart's cravings satisfied. We return again

Notes and Nuggets:

You can use the song "Stuff Mart" from the VeggieTales *Barbara Manatee* CD to drive home this point. As with most VeggieTales songs, this one is light and a bit on the silly side but surprisingly insightful.

Notes and Nuggets:

After having your group answer these two questions quietly, ask them to make a list of possible answers for number two, either on a dry-erase board or a poster. You are likely to hear some of the same answers more than once. This may also be a springboard into a brief discussion of why love's impostors fail to satisfy.

VIDEO

Play "Man on the Street" and "Trivia" before Work It Out.

and again to buy something different, something new, because it gives us excitement for a moment. But then the excitement washes away.

So, what is lasting? What can satisfy the hungry heart? Before sin, the perfect relationships that Adam and Eve enjoyed kept them content and satisfied their hearts. We can conclude that if we could somehow experience perfect relationships with nature, with our bodies and souls, each other, and God, we would also experience happiness and satisfaction.

However, without the engine, it's pretty hard to move the car. Even if we do realize that real happiness, purpose, and love are found in relationships, we find ourselves choosing sin, being selfish, and sabotaging our own joy in the process. We use our free will to choose wrong instead of love. We choose the He-Man sword instead of cake with our friends.

We end up alone. And if happiness, purpose, and love are found in relationships, when we are alone, we are miserable.

What a crazy dilemma! It can seem like enough to make you give up and think there's no point in trying to choose good when the whole system is crashed.

IF YOU ASK ME ...

1. When I crave _____, having _____ instead is an unfulfilling substitute.

2. It seems like many people wrongly think _____will satisfy their craving for love.

But be not afraid! The Bible is called the "Good News" for a reason. In Scripture, God reminds us that "though your sins are like scarlet, they shall be white as snow" (Isaiah 1:18). We are broken, yes, but don't forget that God never stopped loving Adam and Eve—or us—after sin. Scripture also says, "For God so loved the world that He sent His only Son" (John 3:16). God wants us to be happy, to find purpose, and to love and be loved, so He would not let sin and selfishness have the final word. Nothing is more powerful than God's love for us. This is why Jesus came and gave His own life on the Cross—to defeat sin and death.

And the good news? He won.

In Your Faith

"For just as in Adam all die, so too in Christ shall all be brought to life." – 1 Corinthians 15:22

Our faith is full of hope. Even though original sin caused death and separation, Jesus brought life and unity.

When our first parents, Adam and Eve, sinned, we were all affected. We are not guilty of committing the original sin, but we all suffer because of the sin of our first parents. When Adam and Eve sinned, humanity lost holiness and the experience of perfect love (see CCC 416).

Notes and Nuggets:

Break your students up into groups. Give each group a Bible, a paper bag with a rubber snake, a piece of fruit, a wig of white hair, and whatever other props you think appropriate. Have them act out the story of Eden in Genesis 3.

notes

A. Genesis Theater

Produce a Genesis skit. Your leader/teacher will break you up into groups and give you a few props. Your assignment is to act out the scene in Genesis 3. You can reenact the biblical story or make up a modern-day version.

B. Genesis Comics

Make an Adam and Eve comic strip illustrating the lie that the serpent told Adam and Eve.

C. Genesis, Dr. Seuss Style

Retell the creation story through a children's story in a way that would make Dr. Seuss proud. Focus especially on the creation, temptation, and fall of Adam and Eve. Express the truth of Genesis clearly while using your imagination and creativity to make it "come alive" in a new way.

D. Freedom Essay

Adam and Eve misused their freedom, but Blessed Pope John Paul II stated: "Freedom exists for the sake of love." Write an essay exploring this question:

How would the world be different over the last hundred years if even ten influential community, national, and world leaders used their freedom for the sake of love? Which male leaders come to mind? Which female leaders come to mind? Why?

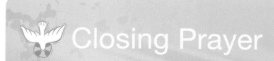

Closing Prayer

Let us thank God for the Good News we have heard in this chapter as we pray:

Instruct me, O LORD, in the way of Your statutes, that I may exactly observe them. Give me discernment, that I may observe Your law and keep it with all my heart.

Glory be to the Father and to the Son and to the Holy Spirit. As it was in the beginning, is now, and ever shall be, world without end. Amen.

– From Psalm 119

Got It?

1. in His image and likeness

2. free will

3. Original sin

GOT IT?

1. He created man and woman _____. (5)
   (five words)

2. God gave Adam and Eve _____, which is the ability to choose. (2)

3. _____ is something like a lost inheritance. (2)

VŌ·CAB'·U·LAR'·Ȳ

IN HIS IMAGE AND LIKENESS:
The Trinity is three Persons united in one God who give themselves to each other in perfect love. We are meant to do the same, so when we are in loving relationships, we understand more about God.

IN THE BEGINNING:
The Garden of Eden is named as the place where God created Adam and Eve. Because we know God does not make errors, the way He created us in the beginning is the way humans were designed to live.

FREE WILL:
God created us with the ability to choose. This ability is necessary in order to be able to love. God wanted us to love Him and each other, so He gave us free will.

ORIGINAL SIN:
Original sin is the loss of the four relationships and a wound to our humanity. Original sin hurts our ability to know what is right, choose what is good, and to love; it causes us to suffer and even die; and it makes us prone to commit sin, even when we try not to (CCC 405).

Objectives:

At the end of this chapter, middle schoolers should be able to:

- Understand the meaning of the language of the body—to make invisible things visible.
- Understand and reflect on the human person as a body-soul composite.
- Confront and discuss spiritual and emotional issues related to the body.
- Reflect upon the meaning of Jesus' being fully God and fully human.
- Interpret the powerful message "spoken" by the language of Christ's own body.
- Recognize Christ as the key to understanding our humanity (*Gaudium et Spes*, no. 22).

Notes and Nuggets:

In Chapter 3, we break open the concept of how the body enters into theology through Jesus' Incarnation. Here, the groundwork for your students' understanding of the Theology of the Body will really be laid. In understanding the importance of the embodied person and the importance of God's coming to us in a fully human, embodied way, middle schoolers will be able to discover the truth about their call to chastity and healthy, integrated development. It is the groundwork laid in this chapter that will enable us to address the topic of human sexuality in an age-appropriate way in Chapter 4.

Tune In:

Your Grace Is Enough — Matt Maher, *Empty and Beautiful*

Anima Christi — Jenni Pixler, *Invitation*

If We Are the Body — Casting Crowns, *Casting Crowns*

Two Hands — Jars of Clay, *The Long Fall Back to Earth*

Note: These songs are available online. Consider encouraging your students to find and download them.

Chapter
Three

Me, Myself, and I
Body and Soul

Opening Prayer:

Lead an opening prayer service. You can close this prayer with something like the following: "Lord, help us, through this chapter, to better recognize the greatness of your love for each one of us and therefore the greatness of the human person. Amen."

Icebreaker

Charades: Invisible to Visible

Have your group break into teams of five or six.

Give each team a matching set of cards on which are written various emotions and moods. For example: happy, sad, bored, excited, surprised, worried, relieved, thirsty, itchy, sick, lonely, mad, ready, or stressed out. Feel free to add your own.

Teams will then appoint a "clue-giver" to demonstrate the clues without using words or sounds. The clue-giver can move on to the next clue only after his or her team has successfully guessed what he or she is trying to convey. The first team to guess all the clues correctly wins.

Use this icebreaker to segue into the Chapter 3 discussion about the importance of the body and its significance in communicating the truth about the person.

VIDEO

Play "Introduction" and "Big Questions" before Story Starter.

Opening Prayer

Leader: In the name of the Father and of the Son and of the Holy Spirit *(all make the Sign of the Cross).*

All respond: In the divine image, Lord, You created him; male and female You created them.

Reader 1: God, You made us good, both body and soul.

Response: In the divine image, Lord, You created him; male and female You created them.

Reader 2: God, You saw that it was not good for us to be alone, so You gave us one another for loving relationships.

Response: In the divine image, Lord, You created him; male and female You created them.

Reader 3: God, You are love, and You made us for love.

Response: In the divine image, Lord, You created him; male and female You created them.

Reader 4: God, You made us without anything to hide from You.

Response: In the divine image, Lord, You created him; male and female You created them.

Reader 5: God, You made us to be happy with You forever.

Response: In the divine image, Lord, You created him; male and female You created them.

Leader: Jesus, You taught us to address Your Father as You did, and so in the Holy Spirit we pray...

All: Our Father...

notes

 **STORY STARTER**

The Language of the Body

My family could have paid rent at church—that's how often my parents made the five of us kids go. We went to Sunday Mass, of course, and then again on Tuesday evenings. Many weeks we also went back on Fridays to pray the Stations of the Cross. And that didn't even include Holy Days of Obligation or other special events like Bible school or youth group.

So it was bound to happen. Sometimes, I would get bored at church. *Really* bored. Hadn't I heard all this before? Didn't the priest say the same prayers at every Mass? Didn't we sing the same songs all the time? Sometimes I was so bored that I was actually jealous of my drooling baby brother, who was still young enough to play with toys during Mass.

That's when the cutting up started. Since there were five of us, I could always count on at least one of my siblings to goof off with me. We would make paper airplanes out of the bulletin or poke each other to the point of aggravation. Before long, my dad would notice what was going on.

This was always bad.

Mom and Dad took church very seriously, and we knew it. When our misbehavior caught his attention, the language of his body was clear: Dad lowered his eyebrows and glared at us with that look—the one that said a spanking would be in our future unless we shaped up. Usually his look was so loaded that we immediately folded our hands and started singing louder than the choir. We did our best to strike a pose that would say, "See, Dad! We're into it! Nothing to see here! No need to think about spanking anyone!"

But if we were too involved to notice "the look," Dad would reach his arm down to our level and snap. Hard. To this day, I still don't know how anyone could make a snap sound so intimidating. The snap always worked. We would freeze, look up at Dad's eyebrows, and pray for our lives.

Now my brothers, sister, and I are all grown. Now we go to church on our own. And now, sometimes when we're feeling brave at a family dinner, we tease Dad by giving him "the look and the snap" for old times' sake.

And then, just to be sure everybody's cool, we say, "Just kidding!"

– Aimee MacIver

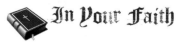 **In Your Faith**

"Jesus bent down and began to write on the ground with his finger." – John 8:6

"And Jesus wept." – John 11:35

"And people brought to him a deaf man who had a speech impediment and begged him to lay his hand on him. He took him off by himself away from the crowd. He put his finger into the man's ears and, spitting, touched his tongue." – Mark 7:32-33

Scripture is full of human persons expressing themselves in the "language of the body." In the verses above, Jesus Himself often communicated through the language of His body. Can you think of some other examples where Jesus' body spoke a language?

IF YOU ASK ME...

1. I know I'm in trouble when my mom or dad _____.

2. When my mom and dad _____, I know everything is okay.

3. My friend, _____, always _____ when he/she is _____.

BRIDGING THE  GAP

Aimee's Dad never needed to say a word to communicate. His look and his snap told us everything we needed to know about his thoughts and feelings. The "language of his body" was loud and clear.

Think about the expression "**the language of the body**." What does it mean? The whole human body can "speak" without words just as clearly

Notes and Nuggets:

For the first two "If You Ask Me..." questions, why not invite your students to demonstrate their answers?

as words spoken with the mouth. We can know if people are happy, afraid, embarrassed, angry, or bored just from what they reveal through their bodies. Our bodies allow us literally to see invisible things like emotions, ideas, and thoughts. Excitement is invisible, but you can see it through the language of your body. When you are excited, your eyes open wide, your face glows, you glance at the clock over and over in expectation, maybe you pace back and forth, waiting for the anticipated moment.

Our bodies also allow us to connect with others in powerful ways. When our team makes a big play or scores points, it's our instinct to high-five each other. When we see someone suffering or in grief, we sense that a hug is more comforting than any words we could say. Not only do actions speak more loudly than words, actions speak, period.

What do you think God created our bodies to say?

IF YOU ASK ME ...

1. I express that I am bored by _____. (How do you express boredom with your body?)

2. I express that I am excited by _____.

3. I think God created the human body to say _____.

TO THE CORE

We may not have a clue what our bodies are created to say, but we sure do have a lot to say about our bodies. Sometimes we complain about the limitations of our bodies. Why can't I run as fast as he does? Why can't I dance as well as she does? Sometimes we even blame our bodies for our problems. If only I were prettier, people would like me. If only I were taller, life would be easier. Many of us struggle to accept our bodies as they are, or we think we would be more lovable if our bodies were more attractive.

All of these ideas miss the truth.

Stained-Glass Windows

A **human person** is neither a soul nor a body by itself. A human person is both. In other words, you are a body-soul. You do not just have a soul or have a body—you *are* a soul and a body! A visible body and an invisible soul are united together to complete each unique person. From the moment God created you—body and soul—in your mother's womb, you are complete only when your body and soul are united. In fact, the human

 **In Your Faith**

This idea of the language of the body is woven all throughout our Catholic faith. St. Paul's first letter to the Corinthians can help us to remember the importance of the language of the body. After teaching us that our bodies are temples of the Holy Spirit, St. Paul gives some simple but powerful advice about how we should approach our bodies: "Glorify God in your body." –1 Corinthians 6:20

Notes and Nuggets:

We use lots of analogies in this chapter to engage the middle schooler's imagination. This methodology itself helps show how invisible realities are understood through visible objects. But remind your students that no analogy is perfect, especially when used in an attempt to explain the deepest mysteries of faith.

The next section illustrates the relationship between the human body and the human soul, both of which are essential to the human person. The body and soul are distinct but not separate. The body expresses the whole person since, in its materiality, it is "penetrable and transparent" (TOB 7:2). It is from this wording that we form the analogy of the relationship between light and a stained-glass window.

Be careful to emphasize to your middle schoolers that they do not just have bodies—they actually *are* bodies. You might have them say, "I am my body ... but I am more than just my body." Ask your students to list information about their friends and then how it is that they know the information is true. Everything we know, we know through bodily interaction. Thus, it is critical to establish the great gift of being an embodied human person.

Notes and Nuggets:

Blessed John Paul II clearly posits that, from the beginning, God designed the gift of the person to be revealed through the body. Consider this passage from his audience of January 9, 1980: "When the first man exclaims at the sight of the woman, 'she is flesh from my flesh and bone from my bones' (Genesis 2:23), he seems to say, Look, a body that expresses the "person"! ... One can also say that this 'body' reveals the 'living soul,' which man became when God-Yahweh breathed life into him (Genesis 2:7)" (TOB 14:4).

Notes and Nuggets:

To reinforce the idea that we do not merely have bodies, but we *are* bodies, consider this statement, which is widely considered to be a sort of thesis statement within the text of the Theology of the Body: "The body in fact, and only the body, is capable of making visible what is invisible: the spiritual and divine. It has been created to transfer in the visible reality of the world the mystery hidden from eternity in God and thus to be a sign of it" (TOB 19:4).

body is so closely joined to the human soul that the body cannot live if it is separated from the soul. This is what we know as death.

Because of sin, we often have the truth totally backward. We tend to think that the value of our bodies comes from how capable or attractive they are. But really, our bodies are not valuable for how well they perform or how beautiful they look. The human body is precious because in its union with the soul, the human person is made known.

Think of a beautiful stained-glass window. When the sun is shining through it, the window glows with colors and imagery. But without light, even the most spectacular stained-glass window is nothing but a dark, blurry shape in the wall. The light reveals the window's true beauty. Yet even though the light gives the window its beauty, the only way we can see light is when an object reflects it. If there were no window to absorb and reflect light, we would never know the light was there. The window allows the light to be known. The window and the light are distinct, but they need each other to be fulfilled.

In a similar way, our bodies are the windows that reflect the light of our souls. Our souls give life to our bodies and reveal our true beauty. And in return, our bodies allow our souls to be known. Without a united body and soul, one human person would not be able to connect with another.

How do you know people love you? It's not because they send you brain waves, or even just because of what they say. It's because of what they do with their bodies. It is the language of their bodies that lets you know their inner feelings and ideas. A hug, a high five, a smile, holding hands, a kiss—these are all ways we reveal the invisible part of ourselves, our souls. The light of love in our souls shines through the stained glass window of our bodies.

But just as Adam and Eve's sin damaged everything else, it was an absolute catastrophe for this closeness of the body and soul. Sin damaged the stained-glass window and blocked the light, so neither could really be what it was meant to be.

How could God solve this disaster? How could human persons regain the truth about who we are and how we should live? Most importantly, how could we ever be able to love? Remember—God designed the body and soul in the first place, so He knows best how to fix them. And remember, too, that evil can't defeat God. God is love, and love always wins because it increases goodness. Evil always loses because it decreases goodness.

God loves us so much that He was not content merely to patch up the damage of sin, like replacing a smashed pane of glass with cardboard. No, God increased the beauty of the original masterpiece. God made the window

Notes and Nuggets:

Pass around a mirror and have your young people describe three things that they see. Read 1 Corinthians 13:11: "For now we see indistinctly, as in a mirror, but then we shall know fully even as we are fully known." Tell the group that what we see in ourselves is sometimes distorted and that it is hard to see the truth about who we are, made in God's image and likeness, but Christ makes the truth of our identity and calling clear. The more we ask God to help us see ourselves as He sees us, the more fully we will also come to know and love God as we recognize His love for us.

even more spectacular, and He plugged in an even brighter light to make it shine.

The same love that inspired God to create human beings in the beginning now inspired a new plan. Even though they rejected and disobeyed Him, God forgave His children. Even though they threw out His original gifts, God gave them something even greater. Sin separated our bodies and souls, but God found a way to restore the union. Sin closed our soul's ears to God's voice, but He found a way to speak the language we best understand. Sin blocked our soul's vision of God, but He found a way to become visible to our eyes.

God became man—with a human body and soul—Himself.

Jesus: True God and True Man

Sometimes we are so used to hearing the story of God becoming man that we forget how incredible this truth really is. God, who has all the power in the universe, allowed Himself to become powerless as a baby. The One who created humans was born into a human family. The One who knows everything had to learn how to crawl and walk. The One who inspired the writing of the Bible had to be taught how to speak and write His own name. The One who rules over all creatures had chores!

God the Son took on a fully human body and soul that is united to His fully divine nature in His one divine person. This miracle—the **Incarnation**—shows us the love of the Trinity. God the Father invited Mary to become the mother of the Messiah. When Mary said yes, she became pregnant through the miraculous power of the Holy Spirit and gave birth to Jesus. Somewhere in Bethlehem, the newborn baby in the arms of Mary was fully God and fully man.

In all of human history, Jesus is unique. He is both fully God and fully human—at the same time. God didn't merely put on a human body like a costume and pretend to go through the motions of human life. He actually experienced life the same way you do. He was eleven, twelve, and thirteen years old. He dealt with His voice changing and finding a group of friends. He felt sad, experienced joy, got angry, cried, and loved people (see Mark 14:33-34; Luke 10:21; Mark 3:4-5; John 11:35; Mark 10:21). He went through the same, sometimes difficult process of growing up that you're going through now, including facing temptations (see Hebrews 4:15).

Why is it such a big deal that the Son of God became human? There are two reasons. First, God was able to make visible His divine love—once invisible to us because of sin—through the actions of His visible human body. On the Cross, Jesus did the same thing He did at the Last Supper and that we now hear at Mass: He stretched out His hands and said, "This is my body, given for you." In other words, "I love you totally."

Notes and Nuggets:

"By his Incarnation the Son of God has united himself in some fashion with every man. He worked with human hands, he thought with a human mind, acted by human choice and loved with a human heart. Born of the Virgin Mary, he has truly been made one of us, like us in all things except sin" (*Gaudium et Spes*, no. 22).

This reminder from the Church about Christ's humanity can help us through difficulty and confusion. Encourage middle schoolers to pray this simple yet profound prayer to the God who has experienced the very same human struggles that they experience: "Lord Jesus, You know better than anyone what I am experiencing. Please help me to handle this situation with peace and love, like You would. By the power of Your Holy Spirit, help me to be like You in this moment."

Notes and Nuggets:

St. Augustine described human persons as coins that have had God's image rubbed out over time. Christ is the "master of the mint" who comes to strike God's image afresh into the coins again—forgiving sins, giving grace, making His image clear and the coins purposeful once more.

Second, the Incarnation also shows us what our humanity is supposed to look like. Jesus lived His human life totally without sin. Totally! Jesus never did even the smallest thing wrong. He never told a white lie, ignored His parents, or had a hateful thought about someone else. Whichever way Jesus handled being afraid, bored, frustrated, or lonely is the way all human persons should act.

Compare how your reflection looks in a pool of water rather than in a mirror. In a pond or lake, you can see shapes and colors, but the image doesn't come close to being as clear and accurate as the image in a clean mirror. But what if the watery reflection was the only one you had ever seen of yourself? You would think that your face was wavy with clouds floating across it! If one day someone gave you an actual mirror, you would be amazed to finally see the true details of your body.

Jesus' life is like a mirror that finally shows the full truth of human nature. After sin, all we can see is a blurry image of who we are and what we are made for. When we look at Jesus' humanity, we finally see the amazing, true details of the human person. These details were always there, but until we looked into the mirror, we couldn't see them clearly.

Remember when we learned that God made Adam and Eve in His image? Humans reflected God, but this reflection became distorted by sin. So the Son of God became human to let us once again become what we are meant to be—like Him.

Mirror Images

Who is the most famous person in the world? Is it the president? An actor? A rock star? An athlete? How did this person become so famous? Most people don't see their own faces on a cereal box. Most people don't hear their own voices when they turn on the radio. You don't get famous just for rolling out of bed and brushing your teeth.

Usually, a person becomes famous by doing something extraordinary, like breaking a world record in a sport, starring in a blockbuster movie, or winning an historic election. Fame depends upon how many other people know and care about what you did.

By this standard, Jesus' life should have just faded away into history. In some ways, he was a regular guy. He didn't write any great books or build any spectacular monuments. He didn't have a huge circle of friends or earn tons of money. He didn't really do anything spectacular.

Or Did He?

It may sound odd, but Jesus was born to die. He could reveal the fullness of humanity only by getting rid of what was distorting it. And so Jesus did the

---

 In Your Faith

*Since we are body-souls and the language of the body is so important, Jesus left us many visible signs to bring His love and grace into our lives. We call these **sacraments**. Sacraments are sensory, meaning that we can see, touch, smell, hear, and even taste God's goodness through our bodies. We don't just think about Christ's Body; in the Eucharist, we actually consume His Body and drink His Blood. We don't just think we are sorry and hope we are forgiven; in Reconciliation, we confess our sins and experience God's healing through the priest's bodily presence. How cool is that?*

The language of Christ's body didn't end when Jesus returned to heaven after His resurrection. It continues through His Church.

Which of your five senses are used in each sacrament?

1. Baptism:

_____

2. Eucharist:

_____

3. Confirmation:

_____

4. Reconciliation:

_____

5. Anointing of the Sick:

_____

6. Matrimony:

_____

7. Holy Orders:

_____

Notes and Nuggets:

This is a good time to show your students a crucifix or, if possible, to take them into the parish church. Ask them to imagine that they have never seen a crucifix before. What is the language of Jesus' body saying? Point out how powerful the image is, even though we often take it for granted. A scene in the film *Amistad* may also be very effective here. The scene occurs at DVD timecode 1:35:45 to 1:39:42, where the Gospel story is told mainly through images. Point out to your middle schoolers that the power of Jesus' love was communicated in and through the language of His body.

Another powerful option is to show a scene of the language of Jesus' sacrificial body from the film *The Passion of the Christ*. If you choose this option, we recommend that you secure parental permission in advance due to the graphic nature of violence that is depicted against Jesus in this film.

Notes and Nuggets:

One citation that Blessed John Paul II never tired of quoting comes from *Gaudium et Spes*, no. 22: "Christ, the final Adam, by the revelation of the mystery of the Father and His love, fully reveals man to man himself and makes his supreme calling clear." In this sense, Jesus Christ is the "mirror" into which we all must look to discover who we are and who God is calling us to be.

Remember this simple
sentence:

The face of Jesus Christ is the
face of true humanity.

most extraordinary thing in all of human history. Because He was sinless, He deserved none of sin's consequences. Because He is God, He deserved total obedience. Yet He faced the opposite of what He deserved. He traded places with us. Adam and Eve chose to be selfish and caused death. Jesus chose to be unselfish and caused life. By doing the opposite thing, Jesus caused the opposite effect.

The bottom line: Jesus loved. He was willing to sacrifice His own life to save us. Remember, His love was not only for His friends. Jesus loved and gave Himself totally, even for the people who hated Him—even for sinners who were throwing bricks through the stained-glass window. If sin is total selfishness, the only way to destroy sin is to be totally unselfish. Love was the only thing that could stop the cycle of sin, and Jesus took love seriously.

Imagine Jesus on the Cross. His arms are totally stretched out in the way that children stretch out their arms to show how much they love you. This much! The language of Jesus' body on the Cross tells us, "Do you want to know how much I love you? This much!" His body speaks—no, shouts—the greatness of His love.

When people say, "I'm only human," they usually mean they have messed up because all humans are imperfect. This can make us believe that sinning is the definition of being human. How wrong this idea is! Just look into the mirror of Jesus and see who you really are and what you really can be. You are precious beyond value in God's eyes. Your goodness is so enormous that God thinks you are worth dying for. Being a true human person is being truly loved by God.

Jesus' body declares not only who we are now but what we are meant to be forever. What happened after Jesus' family and friends took His dead body down from the Cross? They put Him in a grave. They cried. They went back home and tried to figure out what to do now that He was gone. But just as God had promised, evil could not defeat good. Sin could not defeat love. Even though it always had done so before, this time death could not defeat life.

Jesus rose from the dead. He is alive! Although His body had been beaten and broken, at the **Resurrection** He lived again. For the first time ever, death was not the end of life. Jesus visited His friends again, enjoyed meals again, walked and talked and experienced the life of His body again. He remained on earth for forty days after the Resurrection.

In Your Faith

Jesus shows us what it means to be truly human and makes our calling clear! (See CCC 1701, GS 22)

Jesus' friends witnessed Him walk through locked doors and then watched Him rise up into heaven at the **Ascension**. Jesus is in heaven right now but not as an invisible spirit or ghost. He is not broken, but whole and complete—His truly human body joined forever with His soul.

APPLICATION

Choose several of the following Scripture passages and write them on the board.

Give one passage to each small group of three or four, along with a Bible. Ask the groups not to tell each other what their given passages are.

Instruct each group to create a poster that illustrates the message of their given passage using only images but no words.

Have the groups present their posters one at a time. As each group presents, the rest of the students try to guess which Scripture passage on the board the group has illustrated on their poster.

This is another simple way to help middle schoolers understand that the body speaks a language without words. It is also a great way to introduce them to some brief but formative Scripture passages. Challenge them to memorize their group's passage and perhaps offer some sort of incentive or prize for doing so.

- Matthew 25:36: "I was sick and you visited me."
- Mark 10:21: "Go, sell everything you have and give to the poor."
- Matthew 6:6: "But when you pray, go to your inner room, close the door, and pray to your Father in secret."
- Luke 9:3: "Take nothing for the journey, neither walking stick, nor sack, nor food, nor money, and let no one take a second tunic."
- Acts 2:42: "They devoted themselves to the teaching of the apostles and to the communal life, to the breaking of the bread and to the prayers."
- Galatians 5:1: "For freedom Christ set us free; so stand firm and do not submit again to the yoke of slavery."
- Ephesians 5:1: "So be imitators of God, as beloved children."

Remember that Jesus' humanity shows us how all humanity is meant to be. So if Jesus rose body and soul from the dead, then so will each of us. If Jesus' resurrected body is glorified, so will your resurrected body be without imperfections or limits! Your destiny is not just to grow up, have a career, become old, and die. You have much more to look forward to than just seventy or eighty years on earth. Your destiny is the destiny of Jesus—heaven—where you will be totally complete. And remember what a totally complete human person is—a body and a soul united.

What does this wonderful news mean for your life on earth? You have an eternal life of perfect joy to look forward to in heaven. This hope can help you get through the tough things in your life. All the pressure and anxiety of trying to make your earthly life perfect can be gone—because you know you already have perfection awaiting you in heaven. You don't need to panic if things go wrong or if people disappoint you. You don't need to be stressed out about being perfect by earthly standards because the perfection of heaven will blow everything else away.

Does this mean you should blow off life on earth? Should you drop out of school and lay around watching TV if all of this is temporary anyway? No. Every destination requires travel. Your life now is a series of choices that will bring you closer to or farther from your destination.

It is through the experience of embodied life here and now that you will make the journey. Here and now, God is retelling the story of His love daily through our experiences. He is calling all of us toward the ultimate fulfillment. Our call is to learn God's language and to share it with others. Our call is to live as people who have a destiny. The little things we do, like taking out the trash, backing off in arguments with your parents, or defending someone who is being teased, all share the powerful message of Jesus' Incarnation.

You are a human person—a body-soul. You speak powerfully not only with your words but with your whole body. The more you know Jesus, the more you know who you are since He is the "human-est" of all humans. In knowing Him, you know that you are destined for heaven, a place not just for your soul but also for your body.

And these are the reasons you should live out the language of your body, loud and clear, 24/7!

In Your Faith

"One thing I seek: to dwell in the house of the Lord all the days of my life." – Psalm 26:4

Play "Man on the Street" and "Trivia" before Work It Out.

Notes and Nuggets:

If you choose to do the "Human Person Commercials," you may consider allowing for small group work and also giving a few choices as to how the commercials might be made. Some middle school students have the know-how to make videos, while others might be more comfortable making posters. If you do allow for the video option, we suggest setting clear boundaries and also screening work before it is shown to the whole group.

 **In Your Faith**

"Look at my hands and my feet, that it is I myself. Touch me and see, because a ghost does not have flesh and bones as you can see I have." – Luke 24:39

When Jesus rose, He rose up body and soul. He reminded His disciples that, even in His resurrection, He was no ghost. Jesus also ascended body and soul. This should remind us of the importance of living out our faith body and soul.

 **WORK IT OUT**

A. Silent Skits

Make a skit that tells the story of Jesus' life using a song melody and the language of the body only—no words!

B. Comic Strip

Make a comic strip that tells a story without words—only pictures. Trade comics with a friend without telling each other what your comics are about. Write out the story of what is happening in each other's comics, and then compare to see if the stories match what the comics' creators had in mind.

C. Human Person Commercials

Make an ad campaign about being a body and soul human person.

D. My Body "Says" Essay

Answer and explain: What did God create our bodies to say? Why? Use at least one quote from the chapter to bolster your answer.

 ## Closing Prayer

Let us thank God for the Good News we have heard in this chapter as we pray:

O LORD, You know me: You know when I sit and when I stand; You understand my thoughts.
Truly You have formed my inmost being; You knit me in my mother's womb.
I give You thanks that I am fearfully, wonderfully made; wonderful are Your works.

Glory be to the Father and to the Son and to the Holy Spirit. As it was in the beginning, is now, and ever shall be, world without end. Amen.

– From Psalm 139

Got It?

1. speak, words

2. invisible

3. body, soul

4. reveals

5. windows, light

6. increased

GOT IT?

1. The human body can _____ without _____.   15

2. Our bodies allow us to see _____ things.

3. The human person is both _____ and _____.

4. Your body is precious because of what it _____.

5. Our bodies are the _____ that reflect the _____ of our souls.

6. God _____ the beauty of the original masterpiece.

VŌ·CAB'·U·LAR'·Ȳ

HUMAN PERSON:

God created humans with both a body and a soul. We are the only creatures God made in His image and likeness, made to love and be loved. All other earthly creatures were made for our benefit. Every human person is unique and cannot ever be duplicated, which is why human life is sacred from beginning to end.

THE LANGUAGE OF THE BODY:

The major teaching that the visible human body can reveal truths about the invisible human soul, God, our relationships, and how we should act.

INCARNATION:

The Incarnation refers to our belief that Jesus, who is fully God (divine), became man. God the Son didn't just put on a human costume; He really became one of us. He ate, drank, slept, grew, played, laughed, and even cried. He became man so He could die and rise and save humanity from the destruction caused by sin.

RESURRECTION:

After the crucifixion, Jesus rose from the dead. His human body and soul were reunited. Jesus' resurrection makes it possible for all of us to look forward to the resurrection and reunion of our own bodies and souls after death.

ASCENSION:

After the Resurrection, Jesus literally went up ("ascended") to heaven with His reunited and glorified body and soul, where He still lives in a constant offering of love. One day, He will return to earth again, this time in all His glory, to bring us to live with Him forever.

Objectives:

At the end of this chapter, middle schoolers should be able to:

- Understand the relationship between our actions and the formation of our character.

- Understand virtuous behavior is synonymous with truly human behavior.

- Understand the necessity of habit-forming practice for true personal growth.

- Differentiate between the nature of virtue and of vice and their respective effects.

- Appreciate the necessity of grace in the practice of virtue.

- Explore their own good and bad habits (particularly in regard to their use of major cultural forces such as computers, texting, video games, etc.).

- Understand the need for consistency in the practice of virtue, as opposed to having multiple "selves" for different groups and situations.

- Explore the importance of participating in the sacraments.

- Grow in their active participation as members of the Church.

Tune In:

Alive Again —
Matt Maher,
Alive Again

The Motions — Matthew
West, *Something to Say*

***Who I Am Hates Who I've
Been*** — Relient K, *Hmhmm*

More Than Fine —
Switchfoot, *Beautiful
Letdown*

Notes and Nuggets:

This chapter is designed to help middle schoolers see that practicing moral virtue is the means to fulfilling their human identity and, as such, is the means to real freedom and happiness. Often, morality is presented as a set of rules and mandates, but nobody really likes to be told what to do—especially middle schoolers. Moral development requires an understanding that certain actions are in harmony with human nature, while other actions oppose and violate it. God has given us rules and laws, but He has done so for a reason: that we might have life and have it abundantly (see John 10:10). A virtuous life is an abundant life; growing in virtue begets happiness. Unfortunately, we often mistake the purpose of rules as being a test of obedience; in reality, rules exist only to define truly human behavior and thus clarify the path to happiness.

A major strength of Blessed John Paul II's moral vision is his understanding of the connection between human acts and human identity. His doctoral dissertation, *The Acting Person*, emphasized that human acts inform human identity. The Catholic tradition of virtue hinges on this insight. Theology of the Body audiences do not often isolate the topic of virtue but speak often of self-mastery. Undoubtedly, especially in our culture, authentic "virtue catechesis" is very helpful in applying John Paul II's anthropology. Considering the sad underdevelopment of "virtue catechesis" in our culture, this chapter will present a broad understanding of virtue, vice, and grace, which will enable later discussion of the particular virtue of chastity.

Four

How Should I Act?

Opening Prayer:

Lead an opening prayer service. You can close this prayer with something like the following: "Lord, help us, through this chapter, to better receive Your gifts of faith, hope, and love. May these gifts help us resolve to practice and grow the other virtues needed to be men and women of great love. Amen."

Icebreaker

Habits

Begin by explaining that this activity is about habits. Present several statements about various good, bad, and funny habits that many of us share in common. Students will stand and remain standing if each consecutive statement applies to them.

First, say, "Stand if you have any good or bad habits." (All students should stand as this is a universally applicable statement.)

Next, say, "Remain standing (or stand again) if you have the habit of..." and read the following progression of statements. Some middle schoolers will sit when a particular statement does not apply to them; they should stand again if a later statement does apply to them.

- Brushing your teeth every day
- Saying "please" and "thank you"
- Checking your cell phone the minute school gets out
- Watching TV to fall asleep
- Salting your food before you even taste it
- Calling your grandmother "Granny"
- Biting your fingernails
- Washing your hands after using the bathroom
- Wearing jeans more than once in a row before washing them
- Eating a slice of pizza but leaving the crust

- Saying "God bless you" when you hear someone sneeze
- Going to church every week
- Flossing your teeth every day
- Having dessert after dinner
- Waiting until Sunday night to do your homework
- Having an after school snack
- Updating your Facebook status at least once a day
- Sleeping in on Saturday morning
- Hitting snooze more than once in a row
- Praying grace before meals

Students will probably have running commentary as they perform the icebreaker. Take the opportunity to focus on the general concept of habits and how they are formed.

End by explaining that we all have experience with habits, both the good and the bad, along with the simply quirky. This chapter will show us how we can use habits to help us fulfill our true identity as human persons made in God's image, created for love relationships, and destined for heaven.

VIDEO *Play "Introduction" and "Big Questions" before Story Starter.*

Opening Prayer

Leader: In the name of the Father and of the Son and of the Holy Spirit *(all make the Sign of the Cross).*

All respond: In the divine image, Lord, You created him; male and female You created them.

Reader 1: God, You made us good, both body and soul.

Response: In the divine image, Lord, You created him; male and female You created them.

Reader 2: God, You saw that it was not good for us to be alone, so You gave us one another for loving relationships.

Response: In the divine image, Lord, You created him; male and female You created them.

Reader 3: God, You are love, and You made us for love.

Response: In the divine image, Lord, You created him; male and female You created them.

Reader 4: God, You made us without anything to hide from You.

Response: In the divine image, Lord, You created him; male and female You created them.

Reader 5: God, You made us to be happy with You forever.

Response: In the divine image, Lord, You created him; male and female You created them.

Leader: Jesus, You taught us to address Your Father as You did, and so in the Holy Spirit we pray…

All: Our Father…

notes

STORY STARTER

Strings Attached

As I ripped off shreds of Christmas wrapping paper, my heart started beating faster. The shape of the box was right. Could it be … ? Finally? I tore a huge piece of wrapping off the front of the box and whooped. There it was, in all its ivory-colored glory: My first REAL guitar! I was thirteen and flat-out in love—with a Japanese Fender Stratocaster made especially for left-handers like me.

I had wanted to play the guitar for as long as I could remember. Until now, though, Mom had always given me the same old line: "You have to take piano lessons first." But I hated playing the piano. All those practice drills

killed me. I never moved beyond reading the finger numbers to reading the actual musical notes, mostly because I just didn't want to be a piano player. I wanted to be a rock star. So that bright Christmas morning was like winning a victory.

I felt pumped. I couldn't wait. I plugged in my guitar and … suddenly realized I had no idea how to play it. I couldn't really do anything other than turn up the distortion and make loud noise. Not quite rock star material.

But wisely, Mom had given me another gift—five lessons with an expert guitar teacher. At my first lesson, I met my teacher, who had huge, curly '80s hair and wore tight, ripped jeans that might have been cool about ten years earlier. He also smelled like he preferred rock and roll to showers. Still, he was the real deal and played the guitar like a genius. He promised that he could teach me to play, too, if I followed his instructions. I sat down in his little studio with my small practice amp and shiny new guitar, expecting him to show me his moves.

Instead, he assigned boring drills. After he showed me how to hold a guitar, he taught me to play a few notes in a few steps. He gave me the "homework" of practicing the drills all week and said that once I had them down, he would teach me more and eventually how to play a song. I was disappointed. He was making guitar as pointless and boring as the old piano lessons: nothing but practice, the same stuff over and over, and definitely not the rock and roll dream I had for years.

Nonetheless, I obeyed. I played the drills over and over and found they were actually pretty hard. That first week, my fingertips started hurting and swelling from strumming the sharp guitar strings. Then, on top of the soreness, my fingertips developed painful blisters, but I kept going because I just wanted to be a guitar player and was willing to do whatever it took.

The next week, my instructor taught me some more boring drills and a few chords. But then, the week after that, he showed me that the chords I had been practicing actually formed a famous Jimi Hendrix song. I'll never forget that moment when it all came together. I had been learning, week after week, bit by bit, the ingredients to a really cool song. Now, I played it over and over until everyone in my neighborhood was sick of it. My sense of rhythm needed work, so I played every day for hours. Then I decided I wanted to sing and play at the same time. It was a rough experiment, especially on Mom, who had to endure my endless attempts to succeed. It took a really long time, but gradually I could tell I was getting better.

Eventually, I found myself playing and singing in front of people who actually wanted to hear me. I played and sang at coffee houses, cafés, local concerts, youth group events, and church. Today, years later, I play for other

Notes and Nuggets:

This "If You Ask Me..." is another great opportunity to set the stage with your own story or sharing.

people several times a week. How did I go from a guy goofing off with a distortion board to someone who gets paid to play and sing?

I had to correct my initial understanding of what makes a truly great guitar player—it isn't fame or wealth or selling out concerts like I had first thought. The only actual way to become a great guitar player is to play the guitar—a lot. Drill by boring drill. One chord at a time.

Otherwise known as practice.

– Colin MacIver

IF YOU ASK ME ...

1. I had to practice _____ really hard so that I could _____.

2. I don't like practicing _____, but it's worth it because _____.

3. One day I want to be a _____, so I will have to practice _____.

BRIDGING THE GAP

What do a gold medal-winning athlete, a museum-worthy artist, and an honor roll student have in common? It's the same thing that a great rock guitarist, an Oscar-winning actor, and a computer game champ have in common. To become who they want to be, those who excel work and practice hard.

You've heard that old saying "Practice makes perfect." Parents say it when they tell you to remake your bed neatly. Teachers or coaches say it when you complain about solving math problems or running the same old drills for the millionth time. Sometimes practice is so boring and repetitive that you might even wonder, *What's the point of this again?*

Then you get a good grade on a test or win a tough soccer match. And you realize: You couldn't have done it without all those drills or exercises. To become who we want to be, we have to practice.

You have learned a lot about what it means to be a truly free, happy, loving human person. You have learned that your body speaks a language and that it is meant to reveal your soul. You have learned that your ultimate destiny is eternal life in heaven. You have learned that your relationships are meant to reflect God's love. You have learned that, despite sin, God desires you so much that He has given you His very self.

Notes and Nuggets:

This section aims at helping middle schoolers distinguish between knowledge and action. Too often what we know is good differs from what we actually do. At an early age, we learn to excuse this conflict by rationalizing our behavior. At this point in their lives, middle schoolers can begin to recognize such rationalizations in themselves. A good "food-for-thought" activity here is to have your students list in one column some actions they know are good and, in another column, how their actual choices sometimes contradict this knowledge.

notes

All this knowledge is very important because it shows you who you are meant to be. You need to know how Jesus perfectly lived His humanity in order to know how you, too, should live. But it's not enough just to know these truths. You must practice them.

Think about why this is. You could know the entire history of the Olympics, but that knowledge alone would not make you an Olympic athlete. You could know everything about how guitars are made, but that knowledge wouldn't make you a guitarist. In the same way, just *knowing* that you would be truly free and happy in loving relationships cannot make you truly free or happy. You have to turn that knowledge into practice.

Sadly, our world, broken by sin, encourages us to do the opposite. We are surrounded by stuff that distracts us from knowing the truth and then gobbles up all the time we need to practice it. Even worse, we do or say things that oppose our true human dignity because we want to look cool. We don't practice fulfilling our humanity. We do what Adam and Eve did right after they sinned—we hide ourselves. We try to cover up our true selves with all kinds of social masks.

And all of this lack of practice is like training for a marathon by running in circles.

Becoming a young adult is about being mature enough to see how crazy and ineffective it is to run in circles. Maturity means you know the truth and strive to practice it, even if that means making sacrifices. You know who you are as a human person. You know who you are meant to become. You know where you are headed for eternity.

It's time to get real and start running the race.

IF YOU ASK ME ...

1. I know that I should not _____, but I do it anyway.

2. One thing that I know I should do and really want to do is_____.

TO THE CORE

You will never see a dog stealing a car or a horse shoplifting in a store. Animals don't rob banks or vandalize property. Then why do we sometimes call criminals "animals"? It's because car thieves and shoplifters aren't doing what human persons should do. We have a natural sense that some behavior just isn't appropriate for humans. Still, some behaviors are done by both humans and animals, but the consequences are very different because

Notes and Nuggets:

The word *virtue* comes from the Latin *virtus,* which implies great strength. A virtuous person is a person who is strong and healthy in their humanity.

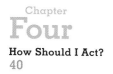
what is right for humans is unique. For instance, we wouldn't arrest a wolf for killing a deer. Yet we not only arrest but also imprison someone who kills an innocent person.

We sense that wrong behavior isn't "human." We also recognize that "right" behavior is especially ideal for human persons. A good person is patient, kind, and truthful. A good person is polite and puts others first. These behaviors and attitudes are the ideal ways a human person should act and think.

These ideal human behaviors and attitudes are called virtues. The more we practice virtue, the more truly human we are.

Virtue is defined as "a strong habit of doing what is good." Because virtues are invisible, they are expressed through what we do in the actions of our visible bodies. For example, you cannot literally see the virtue of patience. But you know people are patient when they have a strong habit of doing whatever they do… patiently.

Remember that a **habit** is something you do frequently, a routine you follow almost all the time. So having the "strong habit" of virtue means doing what is good all the time, not just when it's easy. Virtue grows when you practice it exactly when you don't feel like it! For example, if you are kind to people only until they annoy you, then you don't really have a strong habit of doing everything with kindness. The strong habit of kindness develops when you practice doing things kindly at the very moment you want to do something unkind.

Virtues are different from other good habits like brushing your teeth. When you practice a virtue in your actions, the habit eventually becomes so natural that it becomes part of who you are. For example, if you develop the strong habit of telling the truth, you become an ever more truthful person and the language of your body corresponds to your truthful heart.

Habits, of course, are developed through practice. Practice is the only way to become virtuous. It's just like playing guitar. You need to practice over and over again. You need to do drills and exercises, even when you don't feel like it. But in the end, you'll no longer be a guitar student who needs sheet music to know how to play. Because of your practice, when you pick up a guitar, you'll know how to make music.

Practicing virtue makes us free and happy because it fulfills who we are. A fish will never be freer and happier than when it swims in the ocean, because that's what it was made for. You will never be freer or happier than when you do what is good, because that's what you were made for. Original sin knocked everything out of order, but virtue puts our feelings, thoughts, and reactions back in order, allowing everything to work the way it's

Notes and Nuggets:

To get middle schoolers thinking more concretely, have them brainstorm a group list of virtues. For each virtue they name, have them also give an example of someone they believe exemplifies that virtue. After they finish, point out where on their list the students have naturally brainstormed the theological virtues (faith, hope, and love) and the cardinal virtues (temperance, prudence, justice, and fortitude). If any of these virtues do not surface, add them yourself.

Explain that the theological virtues are gifts from God and why the greatest of them, love, is the only one that remains eternally (see 1 Corinthians 13:13). In heaven, we no longer need faith, because we will see God face-to-face; we no longer need hope, because our hopes will be fulfilled. Explain that the cardinal virtues are the "hinges" upon which all other virtues depend.

Notes and Nuggets:

This may also be a good place to play a simple game of "virtue charades." Divide the group or simply play as a class. One student will draw a card from a stack, on which is written a certain virtue. The student then mimes the chosen virtue as his/her team attempts to guess its identity correctly.

Notes and Nuggets:

In a discussion of virtue, there can be a tendency to focus on "doing what is right for goodness sake," or even to state that this is what will make us truly happy. While doing what is good truly does make us more and more free, John Paul II always approached virtue with much more than an "ideal" (i.e., freedom) at stake; for him, it was always the value of the person at stake. Thus, when he tackles the connection between love and virtue, he probes what makes virtue possible: a person with free will. He explains that the human will must be rooted in and directed toward the good of persons.

Here, Blessed John Paul II makes an important distinction that many young people struggle to understand: "Love as experience should be subordinated to love as virtue, so much so that without love as virtue there can be no fullness in the experience of love" (*Love and Responsibility*, pp. 119-120). As a leader, remember that youth are often so caught up in the "emotions" of love that they sometimes seek such experiences even to the detriment of the other person, whom they seek to love.

As a leader, it is important to help young people recognize that it is not enough to *want* what is "good and best" for someone, but actually to *pursue* what is "good and best" for someone. In other words, we must always prioritize the other person in our search for love, making sure that the good of "us" (the couple) is never pursued at the expense of the perceived good of "you" (man or woman), the other whom we are trying to love. What is good for the individual we love must be pursued ahead of the common good of the couple. In fact, mutually seeking first the beloved's true good will naturally lead to the true common good of both.

If the only proper response to another human person is love, then respect for that person must be the foundation of any relationship. John Paul II teaches us that the only way to "experience" love authentically is to order our hearts toward virtue.

supposed to. Virtue makes what we do on the outside match who we really are on the inside. Virtue is telling the truth with the language of your body.

IF YOU ASK ME ...

1. Three virtues I would like to grow in are _____, _____, and _____.

2. If I _____ every day, I think I can grow in the virtue of _____.

Grace Defeats Vice

Virtue has an enemy: vice. **Vice** is the strong habit of doing what is not good. If a strong habit of telling the truth is an example of virtue, a strong habit of telling lies is an example of vice. Vices have all the opposite characteristics and effects of virtues. Just as with practicing virtues, the more you practice a vice, the stronger the bad habit becomes. And just as virtues can become second nature, vices can also become so natural that they become part of your character, distorting the truth told by the language of the body.

For example, the more you give in to using bad language, the more comfortable you will become using bad language. This will eventually make you even more comfortable using even worse language. And so on.

But being comfortable with your vices is like being comfortable in a hungry lion's den. Even if a vice seems like no big deal at first, all vices are dangerous because they ensnare us in sin. You see, habits are like seeds that grow and spread quickly. As plants in a garden grow, they produce new seeds that grow into new plants. Each new plant takes up more garden space. And where one plant is growing, another plant can't.

This is why good habits—virtues—are so wonderful. They produce even more goodness and crowd out vices! But it's also why bad habits—vices—are so deadly. The more evil increases, the less room there is for good.

Vices enslave us. There is no such thing as a bad habit that makes us freer. Let's say you lie to your parents about disobeying them. Then you often need to tell another lie to hide the first one. Then you may need to tell even more lies to keep your cover. Sooner or later, your whole mind is too busy keeping track of the lies to do anything else. You were trying to avoid punishment, but now you're anything but free. And usually, when your parents find out about your lies, you get a worse punishment than if you would have just told the truth in the first place!

 ## In Your Faith

There are two kinds of virtue we recognize in our faith: cardinal virtues and theological virtues. The cardinal (the word literally means "hinge") virtues—temperance, prudence, justice, and fortitude—are like hinges that a door hangs upon. When we work to practice the cardinal virtues, we open the door to other natural virtues as well.

The theological virtues are faith, hope, and love. They are called theological because they have been given to us by God and direct us toward God. God gives us the theological virtues as gifts at Baptism; we choose to accept and develop them through our thoughts, words, and actions. With faith, we believe in God's love. With hope, we are confident in God's help and His promises. With love, we give the gift of ourselves in relationships.

You may not have as much faith, hope, and love at this point as you would like. Ask God to give you more of these gifts.

Notes and Nuggets:

As you prepare for this discussion, you could prepare a brief presentation on your own patron saint or a saint to whom you have a special devotion. What heroic virtues did your saint possess? Share with your middle schoolers and ask if any of them have a favorite saint.

Everyone struggles with personal vices because of original sin. Remember why this battle takes place—you are valuable and precious to God, so Satan wants to destroy you. But God's love is more powerful if you accept it. Yes, vice is difficult to overcome. Yes, practicing virtue can be hard. In fact, practicing virtue is impossible on our own. Think about how hard it is to break even the smallest bad habit, like biting your fingernails. It's like you just can't stop doing it!

We know virtue is how we should act because of who we are as human persons. We know it takes lots of practice to overcome strong vices by developing the strong habit of virtue. So to make virtue possible, God—who is always there to help us—empowers us with a special gift called **grace**. Won for us through Jesus' death and resurrection, grace is like spiritual electricity for your soul. Without grace, your soul would be lifeless. Grace cranks up your soul with power.

Imagine being stranded in the wilderness and trying to start a fire, caveman-style, by rubbing two sticks together. You would need perfect weather conditions, a specific kind of stick, and very strong hands. Even if all those requirements came together, it still could take hours to produce a spark, which then may or may not grow into a flame, and you'd probably get some nasty blisters. But without fire, you would not survive, so you would be forced to try to do what is almost impossible. Much of your time would be spent on starting and maintaining your fire.

Now imagine how matches would have radically changed your (or a caveman's) life. Instant, reliable, powerful fire! When we accept God's gift of grace, it is like we are cavemen who suddenly discover a box of matches. Our lives change. What once seemed so hard to do before now becomes possible.

Saints and Sacraments

We can look to thousands of examples of saints who have accepted God's grace and triumphed over vice in their lives. There are saints of every kind: male and female, young and old, rich and poor, popular and outcast, ancient and modern. Some saints were outstanding students, while others struggled in school. Some were married and some were in religious orders. But just like great athletes, musicians, and artists, the saints shared in common practice—in their case, the practice of virtue by accepting God's grace.

The greatest way we receive God's grace is through the **sacraments**, especially Reconciliation and the Eucharist. The sacraments are outward expressions of invisible truths which give us God's grace—that sounds familiar, doesn't it? When you go to confession, for example, you see the outward sign of the priest, but what is actually happening is much more

In Your Faith

"Whatever is true, whatever is honorable, whatever is just, whatever is pure, whatever is lovely, whatever is gracious, if there is any excellence, if there is anything worthy of praise, think about these things." – Philippians 4:8

"A virtue is a habitual and firm disposition to do the good. It allows the person not only to perform good acts, but to give the best of himself. The virtuous person tends toward the good with all his sensory and spiritual powers; he pursues the good and chooses it in concrete actions. The goal of a virtuous life is to become like God" (CCC 1803).

than an awkward conversation. The sacrament is like the spout on a faucet that allows grace to flow into your soul as Jesus absolves your sins.

In the Eucharist, by the power of the Holy Spirit, Jesus is really present in what looks like simple bread and wine. The bread and wine become the actual Body and Blood of Jesus. When you receive communion, you don't receive a little piece of unleavened bread. You receive Jesus Himself. That's right, Jesus, the same Jesus who died and rose for you. And the closer you are to Jesus, who always did the right and virtuous thing, the more grace you'll have to do the same.

Them Bones, Them Bones...

Remember that song about how bones connect to each other? "The hip bone is connected to the thigh bone; the thigh bone is connected to the knee bone…"? Through that song, you learned one of the basic truths of human life: the body's many different parts must be connected to survive. If one part breaks down, the whole body is affected.

This truth about your body reveals a similar truth about your soul. Who you are as a human person is not divided into independent parts. You don't have one self for your friends, another self for your family, and still another self for church. But sometimes we act exactly that way.

Be honest with yourself. Do you sometimes say disrespectful things to your parents that you would never dream of saying to your school principal? Do you ever post statements online that you would never say to someone's face? Do you pretend to like movies or music that you really don't, just so no one thinks you're weird?

Any personal trainer will tell you that you cannot make progress toward a certain goal if other areas of your life undermine the goal. Even if you run ten miles every day, you will never win a marathon if all you ever eat is cotton candy.

Once again, this truth about your body reveals a truth about your soul. An important part of practicing true virtue is being consistent in all areas of your life. If you want to become your true self, you can't be a different "you" depending on who you are with. Your character as a human person is deeply affected by your actions. We must make sure our actions match who we are and who we want to become.

The Whole You

You are not a random creature wandering the earth. You are a child of God. How well do your actions match this true identity? Do your actions reveal that you are truly God's child, destined for something far greater than earth?

In Your Faith

The Catechism *says that "grace is a participation in the life of God" (CCC 1997). Wow! Grace is actually a share in God's life. God is free; He is perfect. He is all-powerful and infinite. It is no wonder, then, that God's life in us is exactly what we need to be free and happy.*

Notes and Nuggets:

Some informal discussion questions may bring out some good insight into the common adolescent phenomenon of having different "selves" for different parts of one's life.

1. Who is someone you know who is "true" to himself/herself no matter who is watching?

2. How many of you hate being lied to?

3. Why do you think people act one way with one group of friends and then differently with a different group? Is living this way a form of lying?

4. Why do we respect people who are "true" to themselves no matter who is around?

5. In what situations do you think it is hardest to "be yourself"?

6. What ways are you and your friends tempted to live as different selves?

E.R.

Where do you go in a medical emergency? You go to the E.R.—the emergency room—where doctors heal your body of its sickness or injury. Where do you go when your soul needs healing? You go to the "E.R."—the two powerful sacraments of Eucharist and Reconciliation, where our souls are healed of vice and sin.

E: The **Eucharist** is the source and summit of the entire Christian life (CCC 1324). If you want the power to grow in virtue, go to Mass where you can receive Jesus, the source of all virtue. First, you need to go to Mass at least every Sunday. Also, when you are at Mass, don't just be a warm body in the pew—be really there by focusing and participating! Let the language of your body speak about your inner love for Jesus. After all, Jesus is truly present at Mass. Are you?

R: **Reconciliation** is good medicine for when we fail to grow in virtue. It calls us deeper and deeper into conversion, which is turning our hearts toward Jesus (CCC 1423). We all need forgiveness and healing. We all need help to keep growing in virtue. Reconciliation helps us remain aware of the sins that have turned us away from Jesus and gives us the grace we need to move toward Him again. If we have committed a mortal sin, we should always receive Reconciliation before receiving the Eucharist.

Or do your actions say that you don't care about God? Do you forget about God as soon as the church door closes behind you every Sunday?

It is common at your age to question your faith. Why should you believe in God just because your parents have always told you to? Of course, you should listen to the wisdom handed on to you from your parents, but your faith must be your own to be real. How do you make it more and more your own? By studying it, by being open to it, and mostly by living it. Because who you are is revealed by what you do, the only way you can really be a believer in God is to do what a believer does: choose to believe in God, accept His grace, and follow His commandments. This is how you daily become a person of virtue. This is how you daily become a person of true love.

Following God by practicing virtue is not always easy. You may fear that you'll be labeled a "Jesus freak." You may worry that you won't be able to have any fun. But remember that even Jesus Himself faced fear and anxiety when He had to do what was right and virtuous. Sometimes people rejected or made fun of Him. Yet His great love defeated fear and anxiety every time.

God's love will also defeat any of the fear or anxiety you face when you try to do what is right and virtuous. God's love is always complete and always consistent. God's love is not divided into parts. It doesn't change depending on who's watching. He doesn't think some people are cooler or more popular or more worthy of love than others. God always loves, which is why we can say that God is love itself. You form yourself by what you do. God loves totally, absolutely, constantly—so He is love.

As you grow toward high school, you're at a point in life where you are starting to fill in the blanks about yourself: I do _____, which reveals that I am _____. How will you respond?

Play "Man on the Street" and "Trivia" before Work It Out.

APPLICATION

VIRTUE BEADS

Have the students make Virtue Beads to help them to remember their resolutions and to track their progress. This craft activity will help middle schoolers complete either "Work It Out" option at the end of this chapter.

You will need short segments of leather cord, beads, and crosses. Each student gets a pre-cut cord and a cross. The cross should tie onto one end of the cord, and the beads should be strung behind it.

Then have them tie a knot in the center of the cord so that beads can, with some effort, slide over the knot from one side to the other.

Instruct your students that the cross is to remind us that growing in virtue requires God's grace, not just our own effort. The goal is for middle schoolers to seek out ten actions every day that can help them grow in their particular chosen virtue (as described in the two "Work It Out" assignments.)

Whenever an act is accomplished, have them slide a bead over the knot. At the end of the day, they are to say a prayer using the cross at the end of the cord as they pray for grace to continue growing the following day.

WORK IT OUT

A. Practically Speaking

There are many things in our daily lives that can lead us either to virtue or to vice, depending upon how they are used. Look at the items listed below and think about how you use each one. Next to each item, draw a "plus" (+) sign if you believe your usage of each item is leading you to virtue, or draw a "minus" (–) sign if you believe your usage is leading you to vice. Pick one that seems to be leading you to vice and focus on turning the (–) to a (+) in the upcoming week. Use your virtue beads to track your progress.

- Texting
- Social networking (Facebook, Twitter, etc.)
- Video gaming
- Paying attention in school
- Being honest with parents
- Prayer
- Homework
- Language
- Weekend activity

B. The Virtue Project

Pick one particular virtue that you would like to grow in. Write it here: _____. For the next ten days, you will focus on practicing this virtue. Although it will definitely take more than ten days to establish this virtue deeply, ten days is a good start.

Pick someone whom you consider a good enough friend to help you grow in your chosen virtue. Write his/her name here: _____. Once a day for the ten project days, this friend will remind you about your virtue and ask how your practice is going. You can call, text, email, or have a good old-fashioned face-to-face chat with your partner.

Pick three specific actions you can do every day to help you grow in your chosen virtue. Don't choose vague actions like "Be nice to puppies and bunny rabbits." Choose actual concrete actions, for example: "Fold my laundry when I get home from school"; "Take out the trash every morning"; "Get up when my alarm rings so my mom doesn't have to yell"; or "Stop texting during school."

Notes and Nuggets:

The following assignment is a significant undertaking, but it is well worth the effort. It is a personal experiment in practicing a chosen virtue. The goal of the project is to help your middle schoolers experience firsthand that growth isn't easy—but that it is possible. It can be implemented differently depending on how often you meet with your students. If you meet daily, you will be able to monitor their participation and progress easily. If you meet less often, you may want to send daily email reminders, post it on a group/parent online interface, or ask parents to help keep middle schoolers on task at home. When introducing the project, help your students make a list of virtues on the board. You may want to give them some examples such as patience, kindness, generosity, courage, joy, love, cleanliness, chastity, responsibility, forgiveness, peacefulness, etc.

Throughout the day, use your virtue beads as a reminder and a help for tracking your progress.

For the next ten days, take five minutes each day to reflect on your progress. Fill in the checkbox below once a day.

Day	Successes	Challenges	Strategies for tomorrow
1			
2			
3			
4			
5			
6			
7			
8			
9			
10			

On Day 10, answer the following questions and discuss your experience with your class or youth group.

- What grade would I give myself if I were going to grade myself on how much I grew in my virtue?

- From this experiment, what did I learn about myself?

- In the future, what should I do to grow in my virtue?

- How much did my accountability partner help me?

- What are my overall feelings about doing this project?

 ## Closing Prayer

Let us thank God for the Good News we have heard in this chapter as we pray:

Instruct me, O LORD, in the way of Your statutes, that I may exactly observe them.
Give me discernment, that I may observe Your law and keep it with all my heart.

Glory be to the Father and to the Son and to the Holy Spirit. As it was in the beginning, is now, and ever shall be, world without end. Amen.

– From Psalm 119

Got It?

1. Practice
2. Virtue
3. Practicing
4. Vices
5. Grace, virtue
6. sacraments

GOT IT?

1. _____ makes perfect.

2. _____ is defined as "a strong habit of doing what is good."

3. _____ virtue makes us free and happy because it fulfills who we are.

4. _____ enslave us.

5. _____ is like spiritual electricity for your soul, which makes _____ possible.

6. The greatest way we receive God's grace is through the _____.

VŌ·CAB'·U·LAR'·Ȳ

HABIT: An act repeated so frequently that it becomes a natural part of one's character.

VIRTUE: A good habit that empowers human persons to love God and others freely.

VICE: A bad habit that enslaves us to selfishness. Vice robs us of the power to love.

GRACE: God's free gift of divine life given to us through Jesus Christ, especially through the sacraments. Grace both inspires us and gives a powerful spiritual impact to our good efforts toward virtuous living.

SACRAMENT: Sacraments are visible signs of invisible realities. Jesus gives us the sacraments to bring grace to our souls. Sacraments are administered through the Church.

RECONCILIATION: Sometimes called confession, this sacrament allows us to express sorrow for our sins and have our souls wiped clean. Priests have the special gift of being the instruments of Jesus in confession. When we confess our sins to a priest, it's like we're talking directly to Jesus Himself, who truly forgives us.

EUCHARIST: Sometimes called Holy Communion, the Eucharist is the greatest of all sacraments because it is literally Jesus' own Body, Blood, Soul, and Divinity. When the priest says the prayers of consecration at Mass, the appearance of bread and wine remains, but the bread and wine truly become Jesus Himself.

Objectives:

At the end of this chapter, middle schoolers should be able to:

- Consider why God created different genders.

- Understand the equality and complementarity of men and women.

- Consider how gender identity as a man or woman affects the comprehensive question "Who am I?" (Chapter 1)

- Consider the meaning of sexual identity in light of Adam and Eve's original experience. (Chapter 2)

- Consider how the principle of selfishness versus self-gift applies to sexuality. (Chapter 2)

- Apply the truths about the language of the body and Jesus' standard for truly human behavior to sexuality. (Chapter 3)

- Distinguish that chastity is a positive virtue of sexual purity, not merely the practice of abstinence, and that lust is a vice. (Chapter 4)

- Understand how chastity gives us freedom in our relationships to love and to fulfill our intended purpose.

- Determine how practicing chastity affects daily choices (pornography, "sexting," Internet posting, modesty, etc.).

Notes and Nuggets:

If middle schoolers were the character Daniel from the film *The Karate Kid,* in Chapters 1 through 4 they would have been painting fences and waxing cars. (In the movie, Daniel is instructed to do a series of tasks that seem, at first, to be unrelated to learning karate. Later, he discovers that he has learned all of the fundamental skills of karate from those simple tasks.) Here, in Chapter 5, middle schoolers discover that they have actually been "learning karate" all along. The story starter will illustrate that previous principles have provided the necessary foundation on which they can now build a healthy, Catholic understanding of sexuality.

It is no secret that the Theology of the Body interests young people because it is about an interesting topic: sex and sexuality. The past four chapters of the program have laid a necessary foundation for understanding God's plan for sexuality in a counter-cultural—and even revolutionary—way. By examining personal identity and the overall human condition; by exploring the significance of Jesus' bodily Incarnation, Passion, and Resurrection; by thoughtfully studying virtue, your middle schoolers can now approach the topic of sexuality in a healthy way. This chapter begins addressing your students' already-established ideas, misconceptions, questions, and experiences about mature topics. Naturally, your students may have questions or personal struggles that could arise during this portion of the program. It is a good idea to remind them that you are available if they have anything they need to talk about. Lastly, before beginning the chapter, remind your middle schoolers that a productive learning environment depends upon their openness, maturity, and respect of each other.

Chapter
Five

Sex, Love, and Chastity

Icebreakers

Boys and Girls

Divide boys and girls into two separate groups. If you have a large group, break them into several smaller groups to encourage maximum participation and input from each person. Adult small group leaders can help the activity work even better. Have the boys make an illustration of what it really means to be a man. Have the girls make an illustration of what it really means to be a woman. If possible, distribute butcher paper long enough to trace a whole person's body on it. Then have each group share their work with the other. This activity is also a good fact-finding mission; the middle schoolers' work reveals their preconceived vision, allowing you to determine which topics need special focus.

Opening Prayer:

Lead an opening prayer service. You can close this prayer with something like the following: "Lord, help us, through this chapter, to better see the beauty of chastity and to believe that a life of purity will truly bring us the love and freedom we desire. Amen."

Notes and Nuggets: A Taste of Complementarity

One of this chapter's fundamental themes is gender complementarity—that is, the differences between men and women that bring about something new and wonderful when connected. For a fun demonstration of complementarity, make s'mores or peanut butter and jelly sandwiches. Have your middle schoolers eat each of the elements separately and then experience eating them together. Make the point that while the elements are individually complete, something much better occurs when they are harmonized. Our differences, we can emphasize, bring life into the world.

Tune In:

Needle in Haystack — Switchfoot, *Hello Hurricane*

Love Song for a Savior — Jars of Clay, *Self Titled*

Something Beautiful — Needtobreathe, *The Outsiders*

My Love Goes Free — Jon Foreman, *Limbs and Branches*

Note: These songs are available online. Consider encouraging your students to find and download them.

VIDEO

Play "Introduction" and "Big Questions" before Story Starter.

Opening Prayer

Leader: In the name of the Father and of the Son and of the Holy Spirit *(all make the Sign of the Cross)*.

All respond: In the divine image, Lord, You created him; male and female You created them.

Reader 1: God, You made us good, both body and soul.

Response: In the divine image, Lord, You created him; male and female You created them.

Reader 2: God, You saw that it was not good for us to be alone, so You gave us one another for loving relationships.

Response: In the divine image, Lord, You created him; male and female You created them.

Reader 3: God, You are love, and You made us for love.

Response: In the divine image, Lord, You created him; male and female You created them.

Reader 4: God, You made us without anything to hide from You.

Response: In the divine image, Lord, You created him; male and female You created them.

Reader 5: God, You made us to be happy with You forever.

Response: In the divine image, Lord, You created him; male and female You created them.

Leader: Jesus, You taught us to address Your Father as You did, and so in the Holy Spirit we pray…

All: Our Father...

notes

STORY STARTER

Bee Yourself

Our story begins in a classroom of male students with a male teacher. A bee buzzed through the open window and into fifth-period class. The teacher stood in front, ready to say the opening prayer, when suddenly every boy in the room exploded out of his seat and twenty notebooks went slicing through the air. The teacher watched the bee dive-bomb a row of boys, who ducked in mid-swat, missing the bee. It quickly retreated to the ceiling. The whole class crammed together, each boy trying to make the kill, while the teacher ordered, "Sit down! Everybody sit down!"

Notes and Nuggets:

Depending on your group, this section may be accompanied by some murmuring or giggling since the discussion challenges your young people to a higher level of maturity. Consider reminding your group, especially any who might act up, that you are personally confident in their ability to handle the discussion.

notes

About three good soldiers went back to their desks while the others continued their mission to kill the bee, which they had by now code-named "Operation Bee Sting." The teacher again commanded them to sit down, warning, "Anyone still standing in five seconds will go bee-hunting in this classroom after school. Sit!" The boys knew he was serious, so they sat down reluctantly, only to jump up and scatter again as soon as the bee dive-bombed the center of the room.

Chaos.

The teacher realized the only way to regain order was to terminate the bee. He grabbed the two closest notebooks and, as the bee streaked by him, smacked the notebooks together. Caught between the notebooks, the unfortunate bee fell to the floor. The entire class gave an instant roar of approval for the combat mission accomplished.

A few weeks later, a female teacher stood in front of her all-female class, ready to begin the opening prayer. But then a wasp swooped through the door and across the classroom. Screaming. Shrieking. Squealing. Girls scrambled wildly for cover, flipping some of the desks over in the process. Books skidded to the floor, papers fluttered in the air. The wasp sailed from corner to corner, and each time, the girls stampeded in the exact opposite direction—back and forth, left to right, shrieking louder with every dash.

The only one attempting to swat the wasp was the teacher. But she was laughing so hard that she kept missing. With each futile swat, the wasp spiraled in a different direction, sending the girls into pileups of flailing arms and legs. Finally, the teacher managed to land a solid blow that should have ended the commotion.

Yet the instant the wasp fell, instead of giving a victorious war cry, the class of girls huddled together to peer at the bug lying on the floor and whined all together, "Awww, poor thing!"

Two similar events. Two very different responses. Why?

BRIDGING THE GAP

These two stories illustrate that boys and girls are clearly different. You've known that since you were a toddler, when you decided that certain toys and games were "just for boys" or "just for girls." In fact, this difference has been a major factor in your life from the moment the delivery room doctor announced to your parents, "Congratulations, it's a …!" Your name, your clothes, and even the way people treat you are all strongly connected to your gender—or sex—whether you are male or female.

 **In Your Faith**

In Mark 10:6, Jesus says, "But from the beginning, God made them male and female." It's a simple statement but profound to think about. From the very beginning, God's plan included men and women together. In fact, the very first time God says something in His creation isn't good is when He sees Adam alone and without Eve (see Genesis 2:18). What would the world be like if there were only men or only women? Scary thought!

Our Catholic faith teaches us that from the beginning God made men and women to be a complementary pair. The Catechism tells us that we should all acknowledge and accept our sexual identities as men and women. It also tells us that what is best for society and families has to do with how we grow in our sexual identities and relate to each other as men and women (see CCC 2333).

In our culture, the word "**sex**" is used mostly to talk about the physical intimacy that leads to babies. That's why you may laugh or feel a little awkward when you see the word in bold letters. But "sex" refers to a human person's gender—his maleness or her femaleness.

Think back to the Genesis story in Scripture. In Chapter 2, you learned that God made human persons in His own image and likeness. Right after that statement, Scripture gives us another very important detail: "**male and female He created them.**" That means everything we've discussed so far is affected by sex. What it means to be a human person; the fall and redemption of humanity; Jesus' Incarnation; virtue, vice, and grace—all of these issues in your life are shaped by whether God created you as male or female.

It's easy to misunderstand the difference between sexes. Some people mistakenly believe that men and women are opposites. Others mistakenly think that men and women have to compete to be better, stronger, smarter, superior, greater, or more important. Such misunderstandings can cause confusion and division.

Our Catholic faith helps us to understand that male and female differences are not meant to keep men and women apart but to bring them together. Each gender's unique, special characteristics bring out the best in the other. This is called *complementarity*. Complementarity does not mean that men and women are two halves that together add up to a complete human person. Each individual is a whole human person in himself or herself. Men are not lacking something because they aren't women. Women aren't incomplete because they aren't men.

Think about that classic pair, peanut butter and jelly. Each one is complete on its own. The peanut butter is totally "peanutty" by itself, just like the jelly is totally "jelliscious" by itself. Neither one lacks what it needs to be itself completely. Neither one changes what it is when they go together on a sandwich. But when they're together, peanut butter's best characteristics are enhanced by the jelly, and the best characteristics about jelly are highlighted by the peanut butter. Why? Complementarity!

Male and female complementarity leads to romantic attraction. Eventually, this attraction can lead a man and a woman to love each other in a unique way that doesn't happen with other relatives or friends. Their love may grow into a desire to give themselves to each other in a powerful, intimate way. So they get married and have children, who grow up and experience the same process for themselves.

IF YOU ASK ME...

1. Hanging out with girls is different from hanging out with guys because when I hang out with girls _____.

2. Hanging out with guys is different from hanging out with girls because when I hang out with guys _____
_____.

3. One big misunderstanding that people have about the difference between guys and girls is _____.

4. When we were five, boys used to play_____,
but the girls played_____.

When you were younger, you probably groaned, "Ew! Gross!" whenever you saw a man and a woman kissing. As you become a young adult, though, you begin to see the other sex in a "more-than-just-friends" way. You may feel extremely aware of being male or female when you're around the other sex. You may want to spend a lot of time interacting with the other sex through texting, having conversations online, phone calls, or just hanging out. You may even form a crush on or start to "like" someone.

Sexual attraction is one of the strongest desires humans experience. It's a particularly human desire. Animals do not form crushes, go on dates, fall in love, plan weddings, and promise to share the rest of their lives with each other. Attraction between male and female animals is simply for the sake of reproduction and survival.

God intended sexual attraction between a man and a woman to be much more than that. You may be surprised to hear that sexuality and sex— gender and physical intimacy—have an important place in our Catholic faith. Unfortunately, some people mistakenly think the Church has a negative view of sexuality and sex. But the Church actually has a better, not worse, opinion of sex than the world does.

Why? God designed the complementarity that causes romantic attraction and leads to marriage. God invented the physical sexual intimacy that creates families. And from the beginning with Adam and Eve, He meant for the closeness of husband and wife to be a powerful sign of His love. In fact, Scripture says the special bond of marriage is so sacred that it actually reveals how Christ has a special bond with us, the Church.

And for these reasons, sexuality and sex—identity, maleness, femaleness, romance, physical intimacy—are holy, beautiful, good, exciting...and a *big* deal.

Notes and Nuggets:

Blessed Pope John Paul II considered the spousal analogy in Ephesians 5:21-33 to be a "key and classic text" which serves "as the 'crowning' of the themes and truths that ebb and flow like long waves through the Word of God revealed in Sacred Scripture" (TOB 87:3). Later, John Paul II continues by saying that marriage "corresponds to the vocation of Christians only when it mirrors the love that Christ, the Bridegroom, gives to the Church, His Bride, and which the Church ... seeks to give back to Christ. This is the redeeming love...with which man has been loved by God from eternity in Christ" (TOB 90:2).

While we won't dive into the depths of exegesis with the middle schoolers, it is important for leaders to recognize this passage as the richest biblical example describing the depth and meaning of marriage via the analogy of Christ's love for the Church. Care must be taken when explaining this analogy to youth, as they often interpret information literally, which can be a disservice to their imaginations; e.g., a boy may think that Jesus loves him like a husband loves his wife. Having said that, we want to emphasize that St. Paul describes marriage as a "great mystery," and John Paul II spent much time exploring this teaching. He concluded that while marriage, like any analogy, can never fully explain God and His relationship with us, it is the "least inadequate" analogy for doing so. For more on this subject, see TOB 87-117b.

TO THE CORE

Our culture is obsessed with sex. If you've ever turned on a TV—even to watch a nature show or a sporting event—you've seen commercials that try to make everything "sexy" to keep us interested. Our culture feeds us these images over and over through sitcoms, movies, songs, and the Internet.

But the obsession distorts sex from the way God designed it. In the media, sex—being male and female—is rarely discussed as a sign of God's love. Very few media efforts explore maleness and femaleness as key parts of personal identity, and complementarity is rarely shown. Instead, men and women are often depicted as competitors or even enemies. Masculinity and femininity are even sometimes depicted as choices one makes, rather than the basic truth of the way God has designed each of us.

These distortions twist sex into a source of manipulation, confusion, regret, and shame. What a tragedy—because living our sexuality in the way God intended can actually be a source of union, fulfillment, intimacy, and freedom. Maybe the most misunderstood reality is this: God created sex to first be about who we are, not merely what we do. Sex is first about our identity as men and women created in God's image and likeness, not merely about an activity between a husband and a wife. While many people in today's world are confused about sex, truly understanding God's design for sex takes us once again to the beginning.

In Genesis, after each creature He made, God proclaimed, "It is good!" Stars, water, birds, fish—all were good because they had been made by a totally good God. Then, after God created Adam, He saw Adam alone, and for the first time said about something, "It is not good" (Genesis 2:18). Although Adam himself was good, his aloneness was the problem. God brought many creatures to Adam, but none of them was a good match. As they paraded by, Adam named the creatures but couldn't find in them what he needed and desired—an equal helpmate.

So God put Adam into a deep sleep and finished His masterpiece: Eve. She was formed from one of Adam's ribs—Adam's own self—so she would definitely be an equal match. When Adam woke up and saw Eve, he was beyond overjoyed. He cried out dramatically, "At last! This one is bone of my bone and flesh of my flesh!" When God looked at the happily married couple together, He found it at last not only good but very good (Genesis 1:31).

When we read Scripture, every word is important. So calling Adam and Eve's togetherness "very good" is like saying their relationship is not like that of other creatures. As male and female, Adam and Eve's complementarity

is not just for the sake of reproduction but also for giving themselves to each other in love. Adam's unselfish gift of himself to Eve, and hers to him, brought out the best in each. As human persons, they expressed the invisible gift of their love through the visible gift of their bodies—the physical act of sex.

Think about the reason for the meaning behind such an act. The language of the body is expressed within relationships, depending on the type of bond two people share. You hug your friends, not strangers. You kiss your parents and grandparents, not your teachers. You wouldn't hold hands with your mail carrier, but you might hold your little brother's or sister's hand. Why? Because different forms of body contact say different things. Intimate physical contact expresses a unique and intimate relationship.

Hugging, holding hands, and kissing express affection, but they do not involve the total body. Sexual union, however, is about the most dramatic form of the language of the body that exists. In this way, a husband and wife literally give their total bodies to each other. The language of their bodies says, "We have no barriers. I am making myself totally vulnerable with you, so I trust you to be faithful to me for life, and you can also trust me for life." The language of their bodies also says, "I freely give myself to you, so freely that I am ready to become a parent with you."

What kind of relationship is expressed by this language of the body? Marriage! Sex is the total gift of the body. You give the most you can physically give to someone. Likewise, marriage is the total gift of the self. You give the most you can—your entire life. This is why the total gift of the body—sex—expresses the truth about a relationship only when shared by two people who have made total gifts of themselves in marriage.

IF YOU ASK ME ...

Circle the physical sign that, in your opinion, is most appropriate for the relationship and situation being described.

1. **Grandma comes over for dinner.**

   Fist bump   Hug

   High five   Genuflect

2. **You see your uncle in the grocery store.**

   Kiss on the cheek   Handshake

   Hug   Wink from across the aisle

Notes and Nuggets:

Blessed John Paul II points out that God made Eve from Adam's rib, which also "seems to indicate the heart" (TOB 108:4). They are literally made from the same (equal) material—and they clearly hold equal dignity and human rights. It's good to remind your middle schoolers frequently that men and women are not created to be identical, but they are created with equal dignity.

Notes and Nuggets:

As you continue your own personal study and integration of the Theology of the Body, note that one of John Paul II's most dramatic theological developments is exactly how human persons are created "in the image and likeness" of God: "Man became the image of God not only through his own humanity, but also through the communion of persons, which man and woman form from the very beginning. Man becomes an image of God not so much in the moment of solitude as in the moment of communion [which] constitutes perhaps, the deepest theological aspect of everything one can say about man, ... On all this, right from the beginning, the blessing of fruitfulness descended" (TOB 9:3). Thus, we as individuals with intellect and will reflect God. But we most reflect Him when we form a communion of persons.

The FTFF of Marriage

Marriage speaks a language of love that expresses four main ways that God loves us:

- Free
- Total
- Faithful
- Fruitful

In Your Faith

Our Catholic faith is loaded with the language of the body. Think about how much the body "speaks" at Mass. When you walk in and make the Sign of the Cross, your body is saying, "I renew my baptismal vows and live in the name of the Trinity." You stand out of respect at the Gospel. You genuflect to Jesus in the Blessed Sacrament. Who else would you genuflect to except for God? Genuflecting would be a pretty awkward way to greet your math teacher. Why does Mass involve so much sit-stand-kneel action? It's simple: the language of your body is expressing a relationship— your relationship with God.

3. The bishop comes to your classroom.

Stand up when he walks in the room   Wink

Fold your hands over your head and nod   Genuflect

4. Your best friend gets bad news.

High five   Hand on shoulder

Hug   Head butt

If God made them in His image, then all the parts of a husband and wife's relationship—including sex—are necessary to form that image. Remember that God is not alone or isolated. The Three Persons of the Trinity are in a constant relationship of love, giving themselves totally to each other. A husband and a wife are called to give themselves to each other always, in all circumstances—for better or worse, for richer or for poorer, in sickness and in health. The husband and wife's ongoing faithfulness to love each other reflects the ongoing love between the Father, the Son, and the Holy Spirit. We already know that the Trinity is the ultimate self-giving love. Because marriage is a human sign of this ultimate love, everything marriage entails— including sex—is good and indeed holy—because a good and holy God invented them to express something good and holy: divine love.

IF YOU ASK ME ...

1. How would you express the language of your body to your best friend?

   _____

   _____

2. How would you express the language of your body to your grandmother?

   _____

   _____

3. How would you express the language of your body to a friend with serious garlic breath?

   _____

   _____

Notes and Nuggets:

The following section may cause past hurts experienced by your middle schoolers to surface. There may be some who have already made poor decisions in their interactions with peers. There may be others who have developed bad habits, such as viewing Internet pornography. Emphasize the value of talking to trusted adults about important issues, the value of sacramental confession, and the power of Christ to heal our past hurts.

Some Pastoral Help

Be sure to be sensitive at all times toward the hidden experiences of your middle schoolers, including sexual abuse. Signs of sexual abuse are varied and may include aggressive or withdrawn behavior. Abuse victims may display an unusual interest in all things sexual or have knowledge inappropriate for their age. They may act seductively toward adults. They may, on the other hand, withdraw from the topic of sex and sexuality. The signs of sexual abuse are varied because victims process their pain and hurt in different ways. The best strategy is to be attentive, to have an open ear, and to pray for your middle schoolers. The United States Conference of Catholic Bishops offers more detailed guidance on this subject in its "Charter for the Protection of Children and Young People," which is available for free download from www.usccb.org.

A safe and open environment, along with this program's discussion of sexuality as beautiful and holy, may allow an abused student to feel comfortable beginning his or her healing process. Be sure to familiarize yourself with your diocese's protocol and policy for helping young people who have already experienced—or may currently be experiencing—abuse.

Notes and Nuggets:

Blessed John Paul II points out that the shame Adam and Eve experienced after sin "replaced the absolute trust connected with the earlier state of original innocence in the reciprocal relationship between man and woman" (TOB 30:1). As you discuss the problem of shame driving a wedge between people created to love one another, remain sensitive to middle schoolers who may have been hurt or abandoned in ways that have seriously damaged their own ability to trust others and God.

There is an obvious connection here to our earlier note about signs of sexual abuse. The inability to trust others can itself be a sign of abuse, which causes shame to replace the "absolute trust" that young people should experience with their parents and other trusted adults. John Paul II says that shame can serve as "a natural form of self defense for the person against the danger of ... being pushed into the position of an object for sexual use." But he also warns that "this awareness, unless it is cultivated as it should be, may die away, to the detriment of the persons...and mutual love" (*Love and Responsibility,* p. 182). Sadly, some young people try to compensate for this deficiency of trust on the very same avenues—illicit or abusive relationships—that first damaged their trust and marked their lives with shame. We encourage you to refer such youth to professional counselors, who can help them understand that they are not to blame for abuse.

The importance of helping your middle schoolers place their whole trust in Christ, the One who will never shame them or let them down, cannot be overemphasized. Only in a personal relationship with Christ will "all things" be made new (see Revelation 21:5).

Does This Leaf Look Okay On Me?

Genesis also tells us an important detail about Adam and Eve's fashion choices—or lack thereof. In the beginning, they were naked, but it wasn't an awkward experience because they had no shame—and this was an important part of God's original design for sex.

Shame is the urge to hide or cover up something personal—from God, others, and maybe even ourselves. Shame is about fear and vulnerability. You might feel shame when you get caught doing something wrong, but you might also feel shame when you are "overexposed" physically or emotionally. For example, what if you did something wrong at home, but then your parents told the whole neighborhood about your mistake? You would feel shame—and maybe would want to hide—because something private was exposed to others who should not be involved. Shame fits with our sinful world, where we actually do have something to hide.

However, in the beginning, Adam and Eve had no cause for shame. Remember their situation: God had created them in absolute love and had given them absolute paradise. They had no insecurities to make them conceal personal things from each other. Before sin, it did not occur to Adam and Eve to use each other. They focused totally on loving God and each other, and they did not worry or think about themselves. They were without shame because they had no reason for shame. Adam and Eve did not experience shame about their nakedness because they had no barriers to their loving relationship with God and each other.

Of course, sin damaged this original experience. What was the very first thing Adam and Eve did after they sinned? They tried to cover their nakedness and hide from God. Before sin, Adam and Eve were so focused on loving each other that they weren't self-conscious about being naked. They weren't thinking about themselves. Sin created barriers in their relationship, and barriers make it hard to grow in loving relationships. Think about a time when you met a new group of people. You weren't sure how they would respond. Maybe you didn't want to reveal too much about yourself. This hesitance was a barrier you set up to protect yourself against being rejected or used. Sin brought more than just barriers; it brought distortion. Sin distorted the proper focus of sex from expressing committed love to achieving physical pleasure. Sin makes it easy to misuse people as objects for personal satisfaction, or to misuse the body as a tool to manipulate others or gain attention.

This distortion of the way people experience nakedness means it is no longer safe to be without covering. We wear clothes to protect us from more than just the weather. Because of shame, we clothe ourselves, and this reminds us of something positive: our bodies are sacred and should be protected from anyone treating us like objects instead of persons with great dignity.

In Your Faith

"While he was still a long way off, his father caught sight of him, and was filled with compassion. He ran to his son, embraced him and kissed him." – Luke 15:20

The father in the parable of the Prodigal Son is longing, waiting for his son to return. When the father spots his son in the distance, he cannot wait to show his forgiveness and love for his long-lost son who has returned home. In the same way, God constantly longs for us to come back to him no matter how long we have been away. God the Father is always waiting for us, His "prodigal" sons and daughters. This parable shows the merciful love that God wants to shower on us, no matter what we have done.

Notes and Nuggets:

The following section uses the image of fire to talk about sex. Depending upon your setting, you might want to take the image a step further with a live demonstration. A little bit of fire goes a long way in making an impression! For example, simply light a match or a candle and ask the preteens to brainstorm what things the candle is capable of doing. Of course, be sure that proper safety measures are followed when using fire.

Fortunately, Jesus redeemed the misuse of sex just as He redeemed everything else. Jesus helps us resist the lies about love, sex, and relationships told by the sinful culture of the world. Instead of following these lies into regret and anxiety, we can follow Jesus into freedom and peace. Jesus can heal all. Deep down, our hearts desire the truth about sex and sexuality. And you can definitely handle the truth.

How to Handle Fire

Sex is like fire. Before you start cracking jokes, think about the analogy. The ability to produce fire was one of the most important breakthroughs in human history. Why? Because fire does amazing things to improve our lives. Fire lights up the darkness, keeps us warm, protects us from wild animals, cooks food for us to eat, melts metal for molding into tools, boils water for disinfecting and cleaning, creates the romantic atmosphere of candlelight, allows us to make s'mores, and does tons of other good things for us.

But what about forest fires? And homes that burn to the ground? And serious injuries? Can't fire also cause damage? That's exactly the point! Fire is good and wonderful and enriching—but only in the right place, cared for in the right way. In your fireplace, a fire is cozy and beautiful. But if you threw down some kindling sticks on your living room floor and lit a match, disaster would follow. At the same time, if you tried to stuff that kindling into your couch cushions, you would have an even bigger problem very quickly. It's the same fire, but where and how that fire is handled and used makes all the difference between whether it causes good or brings destruction.

Sex is like fire. In the right place, it can be an amazing blessing in your life. But, used wrongly, it will damage you emotionally, spiritually, and maybe even physically. Sex is a great blessing, but it is powerful and must be respected. If sex is misused, the consequences are serious.

So what is the right place for sex? Marriage. You have already heard that it should be shared only in marriage. That's true. But why? Is it just some old-fashioned rule that nobody really follows anymore?

The idea of saving sex for marriage is certainly ancient, but it is not out-of-date. Sex means the same thing now that it has always meant from the moment God first invented it. When a man and a women share sexual intimacy, the language of their body says, "I am married to you; I am giving my total self to you as a gift." That's a huge statement. Your total self! Think about how hard it is to risk rejection even in small ways, like volunteering an answer in class or saying no to peer pressure. Giving your total self in sex makes you extremely vulnerable. There are two possible responses when you give your total self to someone: you are either loved or used.

So what kind of person do you want to give your total self to? What person can you trust to accept you with love and not reject you or use you? Someone you barely know? Someone you're trying to impress? Someone who will dump you in a few weeks or months? Of course not. And how many people should you give your total self to? Just one—your spouse.

It only makes sense to give yourself totally to a person you are sure is committed to you and who will give an equal self-gift to you and only you. In what relationship are two people totally vowed to each other and only each other? Marriage. Dating relationships have a level of commitment, but it's not yet total. A relationship that includes sexual intimacy must be one of total, vowed commitment—or else what is being said through the language of the body is a lie. And you deserve much more than a relationship full of lies.

So what are you supposed to do about attraction and relationships if you're still years away from marriage? How are you supposed to express your affection now?

Notes and Nuggets:

Blessed John Paul II wrote, "The essence of chastity consists in the quickness to affirm the value of the person in every situation, and in raising to the personal level all reactions to the value of 'the body and sex.' This requires a special interior, spiritual effort, for affirmation of the value of the person can only be the product of the spirit but this effort is above all positive and creative 'from within,' not negative and destructive, ... It is ... sustained long term integration, ... The objection that chastity is merely negative is then incorrect ... True chastity does not lead to disdain for the body or to disparagement of matrimony and the sexual life. That is the result of false chastity, chastity with a tinge of hypocrisy, or still more frequently, of unchastity" (*Love and Responsibility*, p. 171).

As with other areas of life, sex is designed to be practiced with virtue. God doesn't want us to pretend like we do not experience sexual attraction and desire, or just forget about the whole subject until after college. Instead, through the virtue of **chastity**, God intends for us to live and love through our sexuality in a way that matches God's road map to happiness for us. Chastity is the virtue that helps us love ourselves and others rightly through our bodies. It means learning, as male and female, to love as God loved us. The way we express ourselves through our bodies should reveal the actual reality of our relationships. Chastity means telling the truth with the language of our bodies.

Everyone is called to practice chastity—single people, priests, religious brothers and sisters, and married couples. Of course, chastity takes different forms depending on your state of life. In marriage, what language of the body matches the reality that the couple is committed for life only to each other? As the total gift of the body, sex says with the language of the body what is actually true about the relationship. When people are single, dating, even engaged, however, their relationships have not yet reached a level of total commitment, so sex would not be truthful language of the body.

At this point in your life, a big part of practicing chastity means abstinence. **Abstinence** refers to refraining in an exterior way from all intimate sexual activity until marriage. But there is much more to practicing chastity than just abstaining from sexual activity. Chastity means maintaining *interior purity* as well. Having a pure mind and heart is not easy, but it trains us to see each other rightly, always recognizing our great dignity and the dignity of others. This is how chastity helps us save all exterior sexual contact for the right time—and the right time, of course, is in marriage. Chastity enables us to say exactly what we mean to say with the language of our bodies. So it is not chaste, for example, to participate in any activity that causes you or another person to become sexually aroused, which may include things like prolonged kissing. Why? Because these activities say through the language of our bodies that we are ready for more sexual contact. But when we're not married, this is a lie.

Chastity is not about rules just for the sake of rules; it is about the very important goal of loving well. Chastity means saying "yes" to the right action at the right time, which means saying "no" to the wrong action at the wrong time. Chastity means not having sex or engaging in sexual activity when sex and sexual activity do not tell the truth about the relationship through the language of the body. In short, chastity is saying "yes" to the truth of love through purity of mind, heart, and body.

Protecting Your Goal

Think about a football team. A good team needs both an offense and a defense. Both are critical. Practicing chastity in your life right now involves both an offense and a defense. Offense is pursuing your goal of a pure heart.

In Your Faith

A pure heart is like a clean bedroom—it isn't crammed with mess and layers of junk. Everything is where it should be. It is much easier to find what you need or want if your room is in order. In the same way, when our hearts are clean and in order, we can recognize God's presence in every person.

Defense is protecting that pure heart; for you right now this involves abstinence. On defense, you're not just sitting around passively, doing nothing. You're doing something active with a specific purpose. You're protecting your goal of having the freedom to truly love now and in your future vocation.

You might wonder what you are defending yourself against. A main opponent is concupiscence, which is a big word describing the tendency in all of us to sin. Concupiscence is a threat to your pure heart.

Concupiscence affects every area of our lives, especially the way we see each other. This is why an important part of practicing chastity is modesty. **Modesty** is speaking and dressing in a way that respects God's design for our bodies. Telling dirty jokes, listening to sexually explicit music, or watching raunchy movies are all ways of abusing our sexuality, because they distort sex from being about self-gift into being about self-satisfaction. Wearing sexy, skimpy clothes is another abuse. But maybe not for the reason you might think.

Immodest clothes encourage others to look at a person as a collection of body parts rather than as a whole person. Be honest—what do you think when you see a person dressed immodestly? Are you encouraged to see the whole person, or do you just notice body parts? Immodest clothing may bring lots of attention, but it isn't the kind of attention your heart truly desires.

Unfortunately, concupiscence means that, like other virtues, chastity can be difficult to practice. Sexual desire, which is good when we first see someone, can turn into temptation and maybe even sin if we allow our imaginations to go to places they shouldn't. Chastity helps us to remember who we are when temptations arise. It's okay to be honest with God, especially when you are tempted to be selfish in some way. You might say, "Lord, I'm really attracted to this person. Thank You for making someone so amazing. But I know You made me to give, not to take. Give me the grace to treat others with respect at all times."

Chastity also helps us to develop the habit of loving others rather than using them for selfish purposes. Blessed Pope John Paul emphasized that the opposite of love is not hatred, but use of another person—a temptation we can also face in many non-sexual situations. We may be tempted to use our parents for money or our classmates for homework. Chastity helps you see the way you can grow in self-gift.

The vice of **lust** is the opposite of chastity. Lust distorts sex into an expression of total selfishness and violates the language of the body that says, "I am a total gift to my spouse." Lust lights a fire in the middle of the living room. Lust runs around a football field without any particular goal or strategy. And what are the consequences? The house burns down. The team loses the game.

Lust sees people as objects to be used, rather than persons to be loved. In a relationship, lust causes cheating, abuse, insecurity, and negative drama. Worst of all, lust destroys your understanding of your true identity. You're more than an object. You're a person of great worth—worthy of being loved.

IF YOU ASK ME...

1. _____ is a place where I can get modest clothes that I actually like.

2. _____ is a good role model when it comes to modesty.

Notes and Nuggets:

In our experience, many young people have fallen prey to the idea that their identity is established or gained through their productivity: "If I want to be somebody special, I need to ____."

This error has slipped into boy-girl relationships at earlier and earlier stages. As often and in as many different ways as possible, emphasize how valuable each person is because of his or her unique identity. Helping middle schoolers truly believe they are persons of "inestimable worth" (in John Paul II's words) does not happen through reading a paragraph or even through this whole book. Their belief is primarily formed when, through your actions, they see your love for them and your belief in the fundamental truth of their dignity. As Pope Benedict XVI has said, "Of ourselves, we cannot come to terms with ourselves. Our 'I' becomes acceptable only when it has been accepted by another 'I' and is perceived as accepted" (*Auf Christus Schauen*, 90-91). So you help give these youth themselves! Keep up the good work!

The words of Pope Paul VI offer confirmation and insight: "Modern man listens more willingly to witnesses than to teachers, and if he does listen to teachers, it is because they are witnesses" (Pope Paul VI, Address to the Members of the *Consilium de Laicis* [2 October 1974]: AAS 66 [1974], p. 568).

VIDEO

Play "Man on the Street" and "Trivia" before Work It Out.

Notes and Nuggets:

If you would like to use the "Pen Pals" option, see the case studies in Appendix #2 of this Leader's Guide. Choose one, or a few, that you feel would be appropriate for your group. Then allow your students to write their emails to the character which they choose. If a particular person in your group writes a great letter of advice, consider reading it to the whole group as part of your post-project discussion.

Practice Makes "Perfect"

Imagine you want to be a pro basketball player. You would practice over and over again. What if you practiced the wrong way? What if you ran sloppy drills, double dribbled, traveled, fouled, and ran out of bounds at every practice? What would happen during the real game? It's not rocket science. If you practice wrong, you will play wrong.

In our culture, guy-girl relationships have become about bad practice. Instead of practicing true friendship and mutual respect, many dating relationships include sexual activity between people who aren't married. If dating couples can't practice being honest with their bodies before marriage, how will they be honest with their bodies after marriage? Such bad practice has made our world so full of divorce and failed relationships that some people lose faith in love completely.

But remember—love is more than just a feeling or emotion. Love is a virtue. Just like any virtue, love takes work, training, and attention. And to love well, you have to practice well. Relationships between guys and girls are meant to train us for a healthy marriage later on. Sadly, many people view interaction between guys and girls as a game, or as a way of having physical experiences, or seeming older and more mature. But if you practice the wrong way now, what makes you think you will succeed later?

If you want fulfilling relationships now and successful future marriage, practice. Treat others, especially those you date, the way you would want your future spouse, your brother or sister, or even your own children to be treated. Would you be okay with any of them being taken advantage of, or manipulated, or used as an object? Of course not, so set the same standard for yourself. Practice virtue. Find solid Catholic role models to talk with about personal issues and make friends who have the same goals.

The only way to win the game is practice and teamwork.

In Your Faith

The biggest part of chastity is having a pure heart. Jesus said, "Blessed are the pure of heart, for they will see God" (Matthew 5:8). Being clean of heart is more than what we do with our bodies. Purity of heart is how we live and interact with others. It is how we see each other and the world. Whatever captures our minds will eventually capture our hearts. This is why St. Paul encouraged us when he wrote:

"Whatever is true, whatever is honorable, whatever is just, whatever is pure, whatever is lovely, whatever is gracious, if there is any excellence, if there is anything worthy of praise, think about these things" – Philippians 4:8.

WORK IT OUT

A. Growing Up

Think of an adult or find someone in your parish, school, or local community who shows what it means to be a man or woman of God. Make him or her an award of gratitude (or write them an encouraging letter) for being a good role model who helps you to see what it means to be a true Christian.

B. Pen Pals

Select one of the characters in the "case study" that your leader provides for you. Write an imaginary email to them, advising what they should do in their situation. Include three things you learned from this chapter in your advice.

APPLICATION

CASE STUDIES

At the end of this Leader's Guide, we have provided several case studies for use with Chapters 5, 6, and 8. You may select those that you feel are appropriate for your group and employ them in these chapters at your discretion. The case studies are designed to open the door for discussion on issues that your middle schoolers likely encounter on a weekly, or even daily, basis.

Got It?

1. complementarity
2. identity, image, likeness
3. language
4. shame
5. shame
6. sacred, protected, great dignity
7. Chastity
8. Concupiscence
9. Modesty
10. use
11. using
12. virtue, virtue, training

Closing Prayer

Let us thank God for the Good News we have heard in this chapter as we pray:

How manifold are Your works, O LORD! In wisdom You have made them all.
The earth is full of Your creatures. Bless the LORD, O my soul!

Glory be to the Father and to the Son and to the Holy Spirit. As it was in the beginning, is now, and ever
shall be, world without end. Amen.

– From Psalm 104

GOT IT?

30

1. Each gender's unique, special characteristics bring out the best in the other. This is called
   _____. (2)

2. Sex is first about our _____as men and women created in God's _____ and
   _____. (4)

3. The body "speaks" a _____that says something about the type of relationship two people
   share. (2)

4. _____ is the urge to cover up or hide something personal from God, others, or ourselves. (2)

5. Because of _____, we clothe ourselves, and this reminds us of something positive. (2)

6. Our bodies are _____and should be _____from anyone treating us like (4)
   objects instead of persons with _____ _____.

7. _____is not about rules just for the sake of rules; it is about the very important goal of
   loving well. (2)

8. _____ is the tendency in all of us to sin. (2)

9. _____ is really important if you want to practice chastity. (2)

10. The opposite of love is _____ (2)

11. Lust is _____ another person. (2)

12. Love is a _____. Just like any _____ love takes work, _____,
    and attention. (4)

L-63

VŌ·CAB'·U·LAR'·Y

SEX:

The first meaning of sex is about our identity. It refers to being male or female, created in God's image and likeness. Sex also refers to acts of physical intimacy between a husband and wife, especially intercourse. This act speaks a powerful message with the body. It expresses a permanent, total, and free union of love between spouses and their openness to new life.

MALE AND FEMALE HE CREATED THEM:

This phrase in Genesis reveals that God's plan, from the beginning, was for sex and the relationship of marriage to communicate love between a husband and wife.

CHASTITY:

Chastity is the virtue that helps us use our bodies to express love in purity and truthfulness. Chastity requires learning to love as God loved us. Chastity also makes our actions express the true reality of our relationships. Chastity means telling the truth of love with the language of the body. Chastity helps us remember who we are.

ABSTINENCE:

To abstain is to refrain from something, such as abstaining from meat on Fridays in Lent. In this case, sexual abstinence is refraining from all intimate sexual activity until marriage. Abstinence is a necessary part of chastity for unmarried people, but abstinence by itself is not the same as chastity.

LUST:

Lust is a vice that causes people to view others as objects for sexual use.

MODESTY:

Modesty is presenting oneself in a way that expresses the virtue of chastity. It encourages others to see us in purity. The virtue of modesty is presenting yourself with a respectful, healthy focus on your whole person—body and soul—and being careful that how you dress, speak, and act encourages others to love, not lust.

CONCUPISCENCE:

Concupiscence is the tendency or the leaning humans have toward sin. This is a condition that all humans inherited as an effect of original sin. It can be overcome, slowly but surely, with God's grace.

Objectives:

At the end of this chapter, middle schoolers should be able to:

- Differentiate between love and lust.

- Recognize that use is the opposite of love and thus never an acceptable response to a human person.

- Evaluate contemporary culture and specific behaviors with the standards of chastity (e.g., music, TV, Internet use, pornography, "sexting," pre-marital sex, etc.).

- Apply the mandate of never using another person to dating behavior.

- Apply the mandate of never using another person to sexual relationships.

- Determine how other immoral behaviors constitute use of another person.

Notes and Nuggets:

Chapter 5 helped your middle schoolers understand the foundational principles of sexual identity, physical intimacy, and the virtues necessary for healthy sexual identity and relationships. Chapter 6 will now explore how these principles apply to concrete circumstances, especially the critical standard of loving, rather than using, others.

Notes and Nuggets:

Depending on the maturity and needs of the middle schoolers you are leading, sensitive topics such as masturbation, contraception, and same-sex attraction may be issues you deem to be too explicit for your group. However, these are very important topics relevant to the chapter, so we encourage you to be prudent in discerning how to address them. To respect the various situations in which this program will be used, we have included a treatment of these sensitive topics in Appendix #3 of this Leader's Guide. (This text is not included in the student workbook.) Please read the Appendix #3 material before teaching this chapter. Again, consider the age, maturity, and cognitive ability of your students. In some cases, you may consider answering individual questions later or outside of the classroom.

Tune In:

Hold Us Together — Matt Maher, *Alive Again*

Wait for Me — Rebecca St. James, *Transform*

Must Have Done Something Right — Reliant K, *Five Score and Seven Years Ago*

One Real Thing — Skillet, *Alien Youth*

Note: These songs are available online. Consider encouraging your students to find and download them.

To Use or Not to Use?
That Is the Question

The Opposite of Love

Opening Prayer:

Lead an opening prayer service. You can close this prayer with something like the following: "Lord, help us, through this chapter, to be honest with ourselves about the types of relationships we are pursuing. Help us to stop using others and to learn to love them, as you love us. Amen."

Icebreakers

Hearts

On several Valentine-style heart cutouts, write ten to twenty messages from the list below. Distribute the hearts to individuals or pairs, depending on the size of your group. Middle schoolers will share their messages with the larger group, which will then decide if the message expresses true love and why or if it expresses neediness and use. This activity should spark some discussion and maybe even disagreement, all of which serve to open up the critical question "What is love anyway?" Here are some suggested messages:

- I want what is best for you.

- I like being with you because you make me feel good about myself.

- Thank God that you were born.

- I can't live without you.

- If you ever left me, I don't know what I'd do.

- I keep your picture in my wallet and smile every time I see it.

- I stole this iPod for you—I hope you like it.

- You always buy me things. I really like that.

- Where are you? You haven't texted me in an hour!

- If you really loved me you'd do what I tell you to do.

- I saw that you forgot your lunch, so here is half of mine.

- Run away with me!

- LOL. WILL U B MINE? I LIKE U. LOL.

- I prayed for you today.

- You look happy today.

- I wrote your name all over my wall.

- I snuck out to see you.

- You look almost as good as a model.

- If you just lost some weight, I'd really like you.

- If you win the game tonight, I'll be your friend.

VIDEO

Play "Introduction" and "Big Questions" before Story Starter.

🕊 Opening Prayer

Leader: In the name of the Father and of the Son and of the Holy Spirit *(all make the Sign of the Cross).*

All respond: In the divine image, Lord, You created him; male and female You created them.

Reader 1: God, You made us good, both body and soul.

Response: In the divine image, Lord, You created him; male and female You created them.

Reader 2: God, You saw that it was not good for us to be alone, so You gave us one another for loving relationships.

Response: In the divine image, Lord, You created him; male and female You created them.

Reader 3: God, You are love, and You made us for love.

Response: In the divine image, Lord, You created him; male and female You created them.

Reader 4: God, You made us without anything to hide from You.

Response: In the divine image, Lord, You created him; male and female You created them.

Reader 5: God, You made us to be happy with You forever.

Response: In the divine image, Lord, You created him; male and female You created them.

Leader: Jesus, You taught us to address Your Father as You did, and so in the Holy Spirit we pray…

All: Our Father…

notes

STORY STARTER

Three Words

As their two-hour phone conversation came to an end, his heart beat faster. He was going to say it. He had been going out with her for two weeks, so he thought that saying it was expected. Not only that, he thought about her—a lot. He wrote poems for her, texted her every day when he woke up, and changed his Facebook status to say that they were "in a relationship." It was time.

He had never said the big three words to a girl before, but he knew that some of his friends had. He was ready to be mature and grown-up like his older brother. Besides, he had been practicing in the mirror all afternoon.

"My mom says I have to go to bed," she said, and he knew that his moment had come.

"Oh, okay," he said. "Yeah, I should go to bed, too." He felt a lump forming in his throat and his heart bouncing like a basketball in his chest.

"See you at school," she said.

"Okay. And … I love you," he blurted ten times more quickly than he normally talked. Did his voice really sound so squeaky? He felt all the blood rush to his face. Suddenly, he felt very exposed.

Silence. "Hello? Are you still there?" he asked.

"Um… we're only in seventh grade," she responded awkwardly.

He suddenly felt something a lot like the feeling he'd had as a five-year-old when his older brother had popped his balloon. This definitely wasn't the response he was hoping for.

She continued, "Look, I like you and we have fun, but do you even know what love is?"

He hadn't really thought about that. "Of course I do. It's when you 'more than like' somebody. Well, I more than like you."

She didn't say anything right away. "Look, I'm not really sure what love is, but I'm pretty sure that it's a big deal. I don't really have all my feelings figured out yet. I really like you, but maybe we should save that."

He wasn't really sure what to say, but the dose of reality, hard as it was to hear, made sense. "Okay. Well, I really like you," he managed. "Good night."

"Good night. See you at school," she said as her mom came in to say good night.

Later, as he tried to fall asleep, that big question streamed through his head. What is love? He realized that he had no idea. Is it a feeling people develop? Is it a place people "fall in"? If he wasn't there yet, why did he feel this way? Even though his friend didn't have answers, she seemed pretty smart to know that she didn't know yet.

BRIDGING THE  GAP

What is love?

Ask ten people, you will get ten answers. We all know we want love, but it can be really tough to pin down an exact meaning. After all, there are so many different ways you use the word "love." You love your family and you "love" ice cream, but it's obviously not the same thing.

So what is real love? It is the difference between how you respond to things and to people. Think about why you "love" ice cream. It's because ice cream does something for you—it gives you the pleasure and satisfaction of delicious taste. Your appreciation for ice cream is based totally on what you get out of it. As funny as it sounds, you *use* ice cream as a tool to gain some personal benefit.

Real love for people, however, sees that people are good and precious for their own sake. Their worth doesn't depend on what they do or how much they contribute but simply because they exist. Love rejoices in someone's existence and wants nothing but the best for them. Love says, "Hey, I am so glad that you exist. The world is so much better with you in it." Love isn't based on what you get from another person. Real love never uses another person as a tool to gain some personal benefit.

It is tragic how much love is confused and misrepresented in culture. God made things to be used and people to be loved, but too often we get it backward. Do you know anyone who is "friends" with someone else just for the sake of being popular? Has anyone ever been really nice to you, but only so you would do a favor?

Love and use are exact opposites. Think of God's love. Does God value people because of their beauty or popularity? Does God take advantage of people? Of course not. God loves you simply because you exist—without conditions. In fact, you wouldn't exist at all if God didn't love you into existence.

Treating others as objects to control, manipulate, and use is never satisfying and always destructive. Even though sin makes us struggle with selfishness, as a relationship gets deeper, the love should grow deeper, too, and become even more like God's love.

You need to know how real love looks and acts so your relationships can become a mature participation in God's love—and not the greedy, selfish imposter called lust.

IF YOU ASK ME ...

1. Love is _____.

2. I felt used when _____.

Notes and Nuggets:

These points are concisely summarized in the title of John Paul II's early work *Love and Responsibility*, which was published in 1960 when he was still Bishop Karol Wojtyla. In that work, he emphasizes the idea that love without responsibility—or, put another way, *eros* without *agape*—is not really love at all. "The greater the feeling of responsibility for the person, the more true love there is" (p. 131). In short, the degree of love one has for another can be measured by the degree of responsibility one also has for him or her.

Notes and Nuggets:

The following paragraph is a good opportunity to have middle schoolers read aloud. Then, as a discussion starter, ask the paragraph's questions to reveal how your middle schoolers' own experiences show the need for redemption in relationships. Encourage them to do more than point fingers at others but sincerely consider their own habits as well. You may also consider sharing an appropriate moment from your own life when you acted in a way that reflected more using than loving. When appropriate, your prudent vulnerability can help middle schoolers think more deeply about their own tendencies and their need to learn to love as God loves.

TO THE CRE

Two parts of real love are called *agape* and *eros*.

Love sincerely wants what is best for the other person. This part of love is called **agape**. It isn't focused on yourself. Wanting the best inspires us to make sacrifices for those we love. You probably already experience this with your friends. Maybe you watch a movie your friends prefer, or you let them go ahead of you in line. Why? You do it because you care. You want good things for them. When people have romantic feelings for each other, they make even further sacrifices. Have you seen a man take his wife to a "chick flick" or a woman go with her husband to a hockey game?

Love also wants to be close to the person you love. This part of love is called **eros**. You probably experience this as well. You actually want to spend time with your loved ones, not just sit around thinking about them. But *eros* is different from wanting to be close to your mom and dad. In romantic relationships, especially in the beginning, the desire to be together goes into overdrive. You might think about him or her all the time. You may want to talk for hours on the phone—even if you just saw each other that afternoon. You might want to text each other every little thought you have. Obsessive behavior is never a healthy way to pursue relationships. But the desire to be together is good, normal, and an indication that you are maturing into a healthy young adult.

Of these two parts, *agape*—wanting the best for your loved one—is most important. What happens if you have a strong desire for closeness but don't really think about what is best for the other person? What happens when there is *eros* without *agape*?

On its own, *eros* becomes jealous and possessive. It can create insecurity, anxiety, and manipulation. If *eros* never unites with *agape*, love is not focused on the other person but on personal satisfaction. And that kind of self-centeredness isn't real love at all. If you want to be with someone more than you want what is best for him or her, a relationship can get really twisted.

Here is a hypothetical example: Mark and Laura have been dating for a few months. Mark really likes Laura. He has her picture on his wall, he calls her often, and he even writes her poetry. One night Laura tells Mark, "Hey, great news! I'm going to summer camp with my best girl friends." This is great news. Laura has hoped all year that summer camp would work out. However, it means Mark won't see Laura for a few weeks. So he has a choice. He can sacrifice his own disappointment and be happy because he wants Laura to have a good experience. Or he can complain and make her

In Your Faith

The Catechism of the Catholic Church *reminds us that we as human persons are the only creatures that God made just to love and be loved. Everything else God made— like animals, plants, and even angels—was made to do a job or accomplish some task for Him or for humanity. This is why the* Catechism *reminds us that from our beginning we are made for eternal happiness with God (see CCC 1703).*

feel guilty for causing him to miss her for a few weeks. Which response is real love? Which response is really just selfish?

When *eros* and *agape* are properly balanced, love is a true gift of self that says "YOU!" more than "ME." A relationship with the proper balance is like a cooling fan on a hot summer day. The fan spreads cool air outward and refreshes everybody around it. It keeps the whole room from becoming uncomfortable. An imbalanced relationship, however, is like a giant vacuum cleaner that pulls everything inward to itself. It makes things disappear and doesn't give anything back.

Maybe you have seen this kind of relationship. The couple makes others uncomfortable because they are so clingy. They go too far, too fast. They are jealous and possessive. They constantly text, call, message, and obsess. They may get into a cycle of breaking up and getting back together. These are signs of an immature relationship that is about feelings and cravings, not the real good and joy of the other. The relationship is not a gift but like a destructive drug.

Another important part of balancing *eros* and *agape* is the virtue of chastity. As you learned earlier, chastity means expressing truthful language of the body. In this way, chastity protects *eros*—the desire for physical closeness—from becoming selfish. Chastity prevents people from using each other or sexual actions for personal benefit. A chaste person will choose to love, even if it means less physical contact than what is desired. And because God knows chastity will make us happy, we are sure to grow in inner strength and purity of heart when we ask Him for help.

Balancing *eros* and *agape* isn't easy, but it is the only way real love is possible. And who wants something less than the real thing?

IF YOU ASK ME ...

When I think of an example of a good relationship, I think of

_____

_____

✝ In Your Faith

In this famous definition of love, God gives us a sort of checklist to compare how real love behaves with how we actually act. As you read it, ask yourself if you have room to grow in some of these actions of real love. "Love is patient, love is kind. It is not jealous, it is not pompous, it is not inflated, it is not rude, it does not seek its own interests, it is not quick-tempered, it does not brood over injury, it does not rejoice over wrongdoing but rejoices with the truth" – 1 Corinthians 13:4-6

L-71

Notes and Nuggets:

This 'If You Ask Me' exercise asks middle schoolers to evaluate the concept of love as presented by our culture. Ask them to complete the exercise, then discuss the responses. Make the point about how pop culture rarely presents *agape* love but instead focuses on self-centered *eros*.

IF YOU ASK ME ...

Analyze a popular love song and determine whether it describes properly balanced, "real-deal" love, or if it describes unbalanced love full of lust and possessiveness.

Love <u>people</u> and use things.

1. Song _____

2. Artist _____

3. Number of times lyrics say "I" or "me" _____

4. Number of times lyrics say "you" _____

5. Number of times lyrics say "we" _____

6. Which of the following statements best describes the song?

____ This is a total no-brainer; this song is lustful and just plain vulgar.

____ The lyrics seem romantic at first but are really about using someone for his or her body.

____ This song is ridiculously possessive; the artist needs a reality check.

____ The lyrics sound sweet, but if you listen closely, they express self-centeredness.

____ The lyrics express genuine love; it might be great for the first dance at a wedding.

We've Got Issues

Our culture's obsession with sex has very little to do with chastity and real love. Distorted relationships are frequently made to seem perfectly normal. But, in reality, many of the behaviors encouraged by TV, movies, music, and magazines actually cripple our ability to love. They train us to use others.

Just think about how many slang terms for sex don't fit its true meaning. Sometimes sex is called "getting some" or "scoring" or other more vulgar phrases. None of them describe sex as a sacred union between a self-giving husband and wife, do they?

God gave us the Ten Commandments to protect us from this tendency to use others. Yet too often we mistakenly think the Commandments are just a list of boring rules, when they are actually instructions for happiness. Violations of the Commandments—sins—cut us off from real love. The boundaries established by the Commandments are meant to help us

✚ In Your Faith

Our Church loves love! Pope Benedict XVI's first official letter to the Church was a love letter. Just like Pope John Paul II before him, Pope Benedict XVI called us to focus on the importance of God's love. He pointed out that although it's easy to think that God's love for us is only agape—about wanting the true good for us— God also loves us tremendously. Put simply, God is crazy about you! He yearns to be close to you. God desires you so much that He would rather die on a cross than be without you for eternity.

Notes and Nuggets: Pornography

Before reading this section, prepare your middle schoolers. Students are sometimes caught off guard and embarrassed about the topic, so they laugh. Knowing it is not a laughing matter, adults may respond too harshly. This scenario can hinder open dialogue. Try to avoid being defensive. Keep in mind your middle schoolers' age-appropriate struggles to take these matters seriously. Confirm that this is a sensitive topic but that you are confident they can handle it maturely. Consider taking aside any students who could pose a disciplinary problem, and ask for their help in ensuring that the whole group gets the most out of the discussion. Challenge them, but affirm them. Get them on your "team."

As the *Catechism* notes, "*Pornography* consists in removing real or simulated sexual acts from the intimacy of the partners, in order to display them deliberately to third parties. It offends against chastity because it perverts the conjugal act, the intimate giving of spouses to each other. It does grave injury to the dignity of its participants (actors, vendors, the public), since each one becomes an object of base pleasure and illicit profit for others. It immerses all who are involved in the illusion of a fantasy world. It is a grave offense. Civil authorities should prevent the production and distribution of pornographic materials" (CCC 2354).

Notes and Nuggets: Pornography Long-Term Dangers

Footnotes:
The Social Costs of Pornography: A Collection of Papers (Princeton, N.J.: Witherspoon Institute, 2010).

N. Doidge, *The Brain that Changes Itself: Stories of Personal Triumph from the Frontiers of Brain Science* (New York: Viking, 2007).

In Your Faith

It's plain and simple: the Sixth Commandment tells us, "You shall not commit adultery." The Ninth Commandment tells us, "You shall not covet your neighbor's wife" – Exodus 20:14 and 17

The Catechism of the Catholic Church clearly explains God's teaching on pornography. When the Catechism says pornography "does grave injury to its participants" (CCC 2354), this means that everybody involved suffers! The ones who make, distribute, and use pornography suffer. Because pornography uses and abuses everybody involved, nobody is being loved. The language of the body involving sex, which is meant to express love, becomes scrambled and distorted. When God's language of love is distorted, we can easily misinterpret love in every part of our lives. Thus, the Church warns us that pornography is poison to our ability to love and be loved.

know which behaviors will hurt us and which will make us happy. The Commandments show us how to act so that the language of our bodily actions is always true.

Some people think that the Commandments are outdated and don't fit with modern times. It's true that the world has changed a lot since the Commandments were first given. We deal with questions and issues that didn't even exist a hundred—much less several thousand—years ago. But even though the world may have developed, human nature does not change. And because human nature doesn't change, the Commandments are just as important for us today as when Moses received them from God.

The Sixth and Ninth Commandments especially focus on sexual issues. By applying these Commandments to modern issues, the Church shows us that certain behaviors harm our ability to love like God loves. We know you have questions. God has the answers that will help you give and receive real love.

What's Wrong with Pornography? Isn't It Just Looking?

Pornography includes photographs, videos, websites, and magazines that display images for the purpose of arousing lust. It reveals body parts but not the reality of the whole human person. The actors or models shown in pornography have great dignity because they—like all of us—were created by God in His image. Because of this, no one should ever be used as objects or tools. Sadly, pornography mocks, distorts, and hides the dignity of each person involved. This makes pornography gravely immoral, and using pornography can also be gravely sinful.

Pornography is totally counterproductive to having truly loving relationships. Why? It's a way of using people, which is the opposite of love. It trains us to see another person as a collection of body parts for our own pleasure, instead of someone worthy of respect. In pornography, sex has been distorted; it has nothing to do with self-gift and everything to do with selfishness.

Pornography also has long-term dangers. What happens when someone uses pornography? As the viewer uses himself and others as tools for personal pleasure, lust becomes a vice—a strong and destructive habit— that can be extremely difficult to break. Scientific research has shown that a person's brain is changed when looking at pornographic pictures. This means that viewing pornography impairs your ability to bond and alters the way you view the opposite sex.

Some other forms of entertainment have the same bad approach. Many movies and magazines may not be officially classified as pornography, but they still focus on arousing lust. And focusing on lust is nothing more than practicing how not to love. You may know someone who has fallen into using pornography. This is serious. Let your friend know you are worried about

Notes and Nuggets:

Blessed John Paul II defined pornography as "a marked tendency to accentuate the sexual element when reproducing the human body or human love in a work of art, with the object of inducing the reader or viewer to believe that the sexual values are the only real values of the person, and that love is nothing more than the experience, individual or shared, of those values alone. This tendency is harmful, for it destroys the integral image of that important fragment of human reality which is love between man and woman. For the truth about human love consists always in reproducing the interpersonal relationship ... A work of art must get at this truth ..." (*Love and Responsibility,* pp. 192-193).

the harm pornography can do. Encourage your friend to talk to a parent or another trusted adult. Most importantly, remind your friend that Jesus heals and forgives every sin in the sacrament of Reconciliation.

Is It Okay If Some of my Friends Say Sexual Things on their Phones? It's Not Real.

"Sexting" is the more recent issue of sharing immodest pictures, lustful messages, or immoral sexual conversations on phones or computers. You may wonder, *What's the big deal if I'm just goofing around? What if so many people do it that it really doesn't mean anything?*

First, whatever you share digitally exists forever. Once you click "send," your pictures and conversations never disappear. You take the risk of their being forwarded or posted somewhere you didn't intend. Immodest pictures and conversations could be discovered by your siblings, parents, or even your teachers! Even if you don't care now, your pictures and conversations can be retrieved years later by a future college administrator or employer. These are important reasons why whenever someone takes your picture, you should be dressed modestly.

But more importantly, there are emotional consequences and consequences for your relationships. Though texting and chatting can seem like they're not "real," a real personal exchange does take place. We often say things online or by text that we would hold back in real life. Holding back often saves us from a lot of hurt and insecurity. So when you expose yourself in some digital method, you open yourself to being rejected or used by others. Presenting yourself as an object damages your ability to experience real love and can lead others to experience the same damage. God did not make you or any other person to be an object; the only proper response to a person is love. "Sexting" uses others and mocks the sacredness of the body and everything the body is designed to say.

Why Should Sex be Saved for Marriage?

The Sixth Commandment teaches us that sex is for marriage. Unfortunately, some people violate this commandment through adultery and fornication. **Adultery** is sex between a married person and someone who is not his or her spouse. Many people call this "cheating." **Fornication** is sex between unmarried people. Marriage requires commitment and willingness to make sacrifices for your spouse. Having sex before marriage shows that you aren't committed to what is best—God's plan—and that you are not willing to sacrifice your own pleasure for the other person. Even if you do marry the person you have sex with, it will be hard to have a good marriage if you don't practice the necessary virtues. If you can't say no to sex outside of marriage before you get married, how prepared will you be to say no to sex outside of marriage after you get married? Sometimes people ask, "But what if we do really love each other? How could sex be wrong?"

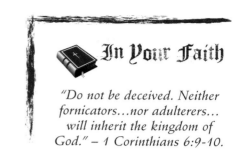

In Your Faith

"Do not be deceived. Neither fornicators...nor adulterers... will inherit the kingdom of God." – 1 Corinthians 6:9-10.

Think it through: In a relationship of real love, you want what is best for the person you love, but sex outside of marriage eventually brings heartache and pain to all involved. Before marriage, the best way to say "I love you" with the language of the body is to save sexual activity until you are married. This is another way chastity helps relationships. Chastity lets the language of the body say, "I want what is best for you more than I want what feels good." If you really love someone, don't you want him or her to have the best future marriage possible?

Unfortunately, our culture sees sex before marriage as normal and chastity as unusual. What a sad fact! Chastity; purity of heart, mind, and body in relationships; and a restored commitment after mistakes should be honored and respected. Chastity alone has the power to say with the language of the body, "I loved you before I even knew you." Who wouldn't want that kind of love? (Check out paragraph 2353 in the *Catechism*.)

So ... How Far Is "Too Far" When You're Dating?

Before we even answer that question, consider this one: What is dating for? While dating is fun and exciting, the purpose of dating is to find a spouse. At this point in your life, with marriage many years away, are you really ready to focus on that search? You may even have more fun and be more relaxed if you concentrate on enjoying friendships and group activities rather than exclusive dating.

But if you do start dating later in the future, how do you show your boyfriend or girlfriend you care? Remember that God's boundaries are never just rules for the sake of rules. You won't find a Bible verse that says, "Thou shall not kiss for more than ten seconds." Instead, based on the language of the body, you can judge what behaviors are too far if they cross these boundaries:

- The language of your bodies becomes sexually suggestive.
- Your behavior tempts someone to lust or sin. Jesus was extremely serious about the evil of leading others into sin.
- You are thinking about how far you can get.
- Your body is becoming aroused.
- You are touching private body parts on someone else.
- You are making people around you uncomfortable.
- Your behavior is focused on stimulation, not expressing love and affection.
- The language of your bodies says, "I am married to you."

Notes and Nuggets:

Some Good News

So often our society's corruption gets all the attention, and we miss truly good news. Since 1991, teen sexual activity rates have been dropping, and now the majority of high school students are virgins.[1] In fact, between 1991 and 2005, the sexual activity rate of high school boys dropped twice as quickly as that of high school girls![2] Among teens who are no longer virgins, two-thirds of them wish they had waited longer to have sex (seventy-seven percent of girls and sixty percent of boys).[3]

The trend toward chastity is well under way, even if you haven't noticed it around you. The National Campaign to Prevent Teen Pregnancy surveyed teens from around the country, asking them if it was embarrassing for teens to admit that they are virgins. Surprisingly, eighty-seven percent of teens said no, it's not embarrassing.[4] Most of those who said it was embarrassing were under fifteen. Only five percent of older teens (fifteen to seventeen) thought virginity was an embarrassing admission.

---

[1] Centers for Disease Control, "Youth Risk Behavior Surveillance—United States, 2005," *Morbidity and Mortality Weekly Report* 55:SS-5 (9 June 2006): 19.

[2] Centers for Disease Control, "Trends in HIV-Related Behaviors among High School Students—United States 1991–2005," *Morbidity and Mortality Weekly* 55:31 (11 August 2006): 851–854.

[3] National Campaign to Prevent Teen Pregnancy, "America's Adults and Teens Sound Off About Teen Pregnancy: An Annual National Survey" (16 December 2003), 17.

[4] The National Campaign to Prevent Teen Pregnancy, "The Cautious Generation? Teens Tell Us About Sex, Virginity, and "The Talk" (27 April 2000), 1.

APPLICATION

Along with continuing to examine the case studies located in the back of the text, you may also want to discuss the "If You Ask Me..." during the lesson.

VIDEO

Play "Man on the Street" and "Trivia" before Work It Out.

Don't Settle for Less

Outside of these boundaries, the language of the body of sex is a lie. The language of the body of sex always says, "I freely give myself totally to you and only you forever and am open to new life." Such a dramatic statement cannot be made truthfully outside of marriage, because marriage is the only relationship of a free, total, faithful, and fruitful self-gift between two people.

But always remember an important truth. None of these boundaries are given because sex is bad. Boundaries are given because sex is incredibly good and that goodness should be protected! When sexual activity is shared outside of marriage, it prevents us from experiencing the true beauty and goodness that is within God's design for sex.

You deserve better than the insecurity and anxiety that come with the world's backward understanding of sex. You deserve the true beauty and goodness of God's plan. Don't settle for less. You deserve real love.

IF YOU ASK ME ...

We live in a world filled with advertising. We are constantly bombarded with marketing messages—think about how many commercial songs get stuck in your head! The following are some popular product slogans. Circle the one that you think would best embody love in an ad campaign and defend your answer below.

- "Let's build something together."

- "Because you're worth it."

- "Obey your thirst."

- "Who are you?"

- "Absolutely pure."

Explain how the slogan you picked embodies true love.

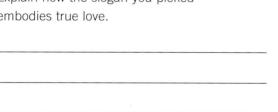

Notes and Nuggets:

"Love for Sale" can be a great way to get your students involved. It is important for you to preview, or filter, what is presented in front of the whole group.

A. Love Story

Pick an appropriate movie that you think is a great example of a love story. Write a paragraph explaining why you think it is a real love story.

B. Love Poster

Create a poster that graphically illustrates the stark differences within the phrase from the "Mind Glue" on p. 71: "Love people and use things."

C. Love for Sale

Make an infomercial for real love. Show how lust and use leave people miserable and unhappy and then how love fulfills us.

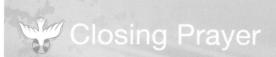 Closing Prayer

Let us thank God for the Good News we have heard in this chapter as we pray:

Only in God is my soul at rest; from Him comes my salvation; from Him comes my hope. He only is my rock and my salvation. I shall not be disturbed.

Glory be to the Father and to the Son and to the Holy Spirit. As it was in the beginning, is now, and ever shall be, world without end. Amen.

– From Psalm 62

Got It?

1. loved, used
2. use
3. agape
4. eros
5. Adultery
6. Fornication

GOT IT?

1. God made people to be _____ and things to be _____. *3*

2. Real love is the opposite of _____. *2*

3. Love sincerely wants what is best for other persons. This part of love is called _____. *2*

4. Love also wants to be close to the person you are attracted to. This part of love is called _____. *2*

5. _____ is sex between a married person and someone who is not his or her spouse. *2*

6. _____ is when unmarried people have sex. *2*

VŌ·CAB'·U·LAR'·Ȳ

AGAPE:
Agape is the totally selfless part of love that wants what is truly best for your loved one and works to achieve it. *Agape* seeks nothing in return; it is pure charity and selflessness.

EROS:
Eros is the part of love that makes you desire to be united with your loved one. *Eros* must always be filled with *agape* so that it can bring people into truly loving union instead of selfishness or possessiveness.

ADULTERY:
Sexual activity between a married person and someone who is not his or her spouse.

FORNICATION:
Sexual activity between people who are not married.

PORNOGRAPHY:
Photographs, videos, websites, and magazines that display sexual poses, acts, and body parts for the purpose of arousing lust.

Objectives:

At the end of this chapter, middle schoolers should be able to:

- Explain the universal vocation to holiness and the particular vocations to marriage, consecrated life, and ordained life.

- Identify flaws in the secular understanding of dating.

- Understand the universal call to holiness.

- Consider how to live the universal vocation to holiness in their daily lives.

Notes and Nuggets:

The early stages of adolescence are critical in vocational discernment. Although few middle schoolers know their specific, lifelong calling, the impressions they form now remain deeply rooted. Therefore, the present moment is pivotal for encouraging openness to God's plan, including the possibility of priesthood or consecrated life. The vocation for most, of course, will be marriage. It is critical to help your students see that anyone can say they are open to God's will, but actually being open to God's will means being open to all the possibilities of His will. Point out that God would never call them to a vocation that makes them miserable; in fact, their true vocation will allow them to truly become themselves. Most importantly, middle schoolers need to recognize that because everyone is called to sanctity, all vocations are holy—and that their own personal vocation is to be holy as well.

Tune In:

Made to Love — TobyMac, *Portable Sounds*

Wait and See — Brandon Heath, *What If We*

It's Your Life — Francesca Batistelli, *My Paper Heart*

Quiet Enough — Righteous B, *How a Wound Bleeds*

Note: These songs are available online. Consider encouraging your students to find and download them.

Chapter Seven

Vocation
God's Call, My Response

Opening Prayer:

Lead an opening prayer service. You can close this prayer with something like the following: "Lord, help us, through this chapter, to learn to trust You more fully and to be honest with You about our hopes and dreams. Help us to trust that You have great plans for our lives and that You want us to be happy even more than we want to be happy. Help us to prayerfully prepare for whichever vocation You have in mind for us. Amen."

Icebreaker

The Calling

Have one volunteer stand on one side of the room and another stand at the opposite side. One volunteer will play the role of God and the other will play the role of a Christian. Have about seven students stand in between them. (To increase participation, you could do seven pairs.) Then give the following written message to "God": "Before I formed you in the womb I knew you. A prophet to the nations I have appointed you." Tell "God" that when you give the signal, "God" should communicate the message to the "Christian" at the opposite side of the room by softly repeating the message. Meanwhile, give the middle schoolers between "God" and the "Christian" the following messages:

"Buy this, you'll like it!"

"LOL... BRB... JK... IDK..."

"This just in... blah, blah, blah, blah."

"And if you act now, you'll get this free book light!"

"La la la la la la..."

"Text me! Call me!"

"Hey, check out my Facebook status!"

Instruct the students to keep repeating their messages until you tap them on the shoulder. (When you tap their shoulders, they should become still and silent.) The room will become quite noisy. At the peak of the noise, ask the listening "Christian" what "God" is saying. Then one by one, silence the students between "God" and the "Christian" by tapping their shoulders. Once only "God" is speaking, His message should be clear and easy to understand. Ask the "Christian" what the message is again.

Explain that we live in a noisy world, and all the noise can make it really difficult to hear God's voice. In fact, our world is so noisy that we often don't believe God is speaking to us at all. Note that silence and attentive listening can help us to hear God's message.

An option would be to have "God" pass on the message by whispering it to the middle schoolers between "God" and the "Christian" who will then repeat it to the "Christian." Explain the analogy: others can help us to hear God's message as well.

VIDEO

Play "Introduction" and "Big Questions" before Story Starter.

Opening Prayer

Leader: In the name of the Father and of the Son and of the Holy Spirit *(all make the Sign of the Cross).*

All respond: In the divine image, Lord, You created him; male and female You created them.

Reader 1: God, You made us good, both body and soul.

Response: In the divine image, Lord, You created him; male and female You created them.

Reader 2: God, You saw that it was not good for us to be alone, so You gave us one another for loving relationships.

Response: In the divine image, Lord, You created him; male and female You created them.

Reader 3: God, You are love, and You made us for love.

Response: In the divine image, Lord, You created him; male and female You created them.

Reader 4: God, You made us without anything to hide from You.

Response: In the divine image, Lord, You created him; male and female You created them.

Reader 5: God, You made us to be happy with You forever.

Response: In the divine image, Lord, You created him; male and female You created them.

Leader: Jesus, You taught us to address Your Father as You did, and so in the Holy Spirit we pray…

All: Our Father…

notes

STORY STARTER

Holy Matrimony

The day Aimee and I got married was the best day of my life. I know people always say that, but this really was. At 8:30 a.m., my best friend, Greg, woke me up at the hotel where we were staying with several other friends. I jumped up, excited to put on my tuxedo. With my red hair and scruffy beard, I ended up looking like a cross between James Bond and the Lucky Charms leprechaun.

But I had way too much nervous energy just to hang out at the hotel. I asked my best man to drive me to the Eucharistic adoration chapel where I had proposed to my future wife nine months before. There I knelt down,

had a good heart-to-heart chat with God, and tried to prepare for the big moment.

We left the chapel and headed to the church, but there were still a few hours until the wedding began. Every minute seemed like ten. I could hardly wait! I paced. I prayed. I waited… and waited… and waited. Finally, guests started arriving. I headed to my position and watched as people filled the church. Before I knew it, I was standing next to Greg as music played and bridesmaids started strolling down the aisle.

Then—a burst of light! The heavy church door opened. It was better than a vision in any Hollywood movie when I saw my beautiful bride make her entrance on her father's arm. With every step they took down the aisle, my heart beat faster until she was finally only two feet away. Her father reached out to shake my hand, but then he stopped. Instead of the traditional short handshake, he put something cool and metallic in the palm of my hand and began to speak.

"There was once a husband who loved his bride so much that he would do anything for her. Anything." I knew his words were intense and serious, but they didn't really register at first. When he let go of my hand, I looked down to see the object he had placed in my palm.

It was a small silver crucifix. Suddenly I understood. The husband was Jesus, the bride was the Church, and He had done not only anything, but everything, for her. He gave His life in love. And this was the same reason I stood at the altar that day, to lay down my life in love for my bride. What an awesome call to be like Christ to the person I love most—awesome and holy.

– Colin MacIver

BRIDGING THE  GAP

Have you ever thought about your parents or other married people as holy? What about your friends? What about yourself?

The idea that only a few special people are supposed to be holy is common. Many people never think about marriage as holy. Often, we think holiness is something for priests and nuns, not regular people or typical families. Priests and nuns are supposed to be holy—it's their job, isn't it?

But Jesus never said anything like that. He said without limits, "Follow me." He called all kinds of people to holiness. This makes sense if we understand what holiness really is. It's not wearing a "Jesus t-shirt" or praying twenty

rosaries every day. Holy means "reserved for" or "dedicated." And we all should be reserved for and dedicated to God, right?

Every call from God is a call to holiness. This call is known as a **vocation**. Vocation means simply "a call from God." So whether God calls you to become a priest, monk, nun, husband, or wife, every human person on the planet has a vocation to holiness.

A reporter once asked Blessed Mother Teresa of Calcutta to define holiness. She said, "Holiness is not a luxury for a few, but a simple duty for you and me."

You have a vocation to holiness, too. That doesn't mean you have to wear a giant cross or preach on the sidewalk, although you are welcome to do both. Your vocation to holiness means simply to become the best you, "Saint Me," that God is calling you to become to prepare you ultimately to be with Him in heaven forever. In exactly the same way Jesus called St. Peter and St. Mary Magdalene, He calls you right now: "Follow Me."

But don't think that your vocation is something for later or that you can just worry about "God stuff" when you're older. Your vocation starts now. You are called to be holy in your daily life as a student, as a friend, and as a son or daughter in your family. Every day when you wake up, you have the choice to become more you and grow closer to God (and heaven), or to become less of yourself and move farther away from Him. God is inviting you to say yes to holiness right now—and for the rest of your life.

IF YOU ASK ME ...

1. Someone I know who lives their vocation to holiness: _____
_____.

2. I would grow in holiness if I _____ .

TO THE CORE

In this program, you have done some pretty intense thinking—about your identity; your weaknesses and strengths; what it means to be human; virtue and vice; and sexuality and relationships. All are part of fulfilling your vocation to holiness and becoming the saint God made you to be.

You may think it sounds scary to be a saint. You may be afraid that sainthood would mean losing your identity and living a boring, cookie-cutter life. The truth is that the closer you get to God, the more you become yourself. Sainthood is when your individuality reaches its perfection. It's not about being put into a mold. On the contrary, it's the unique, full bloom of

your personality. For example, St. John Bosco and St. Teresa of Avila were both known to be practical jokers. As a little girl, St. Thérèse and her friends walked around town pretending to be blind beggars until they accidentally knocked over a bunch of oranges at a produce market. St. Joseph Cupertino used to randomly levitate. St. Joan of Arc led the French army to victory in battle when she was only a teenager. Do these sound like boring, typical lives? It is sin that dulls our individuality.

The other aspect of your personal vocation is God's call to a particular way of life within the Church—to be married; consecrated as a nun, sister, consecrated single, monk, or religious brother; or ordained as a deacon or priest. All vocations are important signs of Jesus' love for the Church. All are ways to become a saint. And all vocations require us to give ourselves unselfishly in love.

Marriage

The most common vocation is **marriage**. In marriage, a man and a woman exchange vows that make their relationship a great sign of God's love. First, they promise to give themselves only to each other until death. This lifelong commitment is a reminder of God's eternal love for us. They also promise to accept any children that God sends as a gift. This family love is a reminder of God's life-giving love and of how precious every human person is to God.

These wedding promises are the most important part of the sacrament of Matrimony—much more important than the flowers, dress, tuxedo, and cake—because they are the most important part of marriage. The whole purpose of marriage is to stay committed to your spouse, who should always come first. If a couple doesn't want to stay together for the rest of their lives, or if they don't want to be open to children, they can't live out the ultimate meaning of marriage.

In Scripture, St. Paul's Letter to the Ephesians discusses that ultimate meaning. He calls marriage "a great mystery." It is not just about a man and a woman, but actually about Christ and the Church. In other words, marriage is much more than a couple signing a legal contract or agreeing to share a household. A husband and wife are called to be a visible reminder of the profound love that Jesus has for His Bride, the Church, which is especially revealed in His Passion and Resurrection.

When a husband and wife enter marriage with unselfish love, their home becomes like a little Church. And because their vocation is holy, the everyday tasks of marriage and family—like doing laundry and mowing the lawn and even changing diapers—become holy too. Husbands and wives can become great saints just by living out their vocation with love.

In Your Faith

"The Church and the world today more than ever need married couples and families who generously let themselves be schooled by Christ."
– Blessed Pope John Paul II

"Religious orders are not formed for the purpose of gathering perfect people, but for those who have the courage to aim for perfection."
– St. Francis de Sales

IF YOU ASK ME …

_____ and _____ are a good example of married life to me.

Consecrated Life

Another vocation is **consecrated life** as a religious sister, a nun, a religious brother, or even as a consecrated single person. Consecrated people make vows, too, but to God instead of to a husband or wife. Consecrated people vow not to have an earthly marriage or many earthly possessions so that they will have more time, energy, and focus to do special work for God, such as serving the poor, running hospitals, traveling as missionaries, or praying daily for the pope and the entire Church. People in consecrated life usually live in a community with other people who have made the same vows. There are hundreds of different orders, different communities with distinct ways of life, each fulfilling a different need in the Church.

Consecrated life requires an unselfish gift of self to others. Like marriage, consecrated life is a type of lifelong commitment. This is why a nun wears a veil—to symbolize that she is the "bride" of Christ Himself rather than the bride of an earthly husband. This close union with Jesus is like a sneak preview of heaven, where we will all be united intimately with God.

Overview of Consecrated Life

There are many forms of consecrated life, so describing them all can get complicated! Here is a brief overview. Sisters, nuns, monks, brothers, and religious-order priests are all referred to as being part of _religious life._ In religious life, a community of brothers or sisters lives, works, prays, and even has fun together. If you feel interested in consecrated life, talk to someone who is living out that vocation.

Others live out the consecrated vocation as _consecrated virgins_, members of _secular institutes,_ or in other forms. They may or may not live in community with others, but they all commit themselves to their bishop and serve the Church specifically as a consecrated single person in the world. All those called to consecrated life live out their call to love in a way that is entirely dedicated to Christ and the Church, reminding us all that we are destined for heaven. Celibates aren't people who couldn't find a spouse. Instead, they choose to consecrate themselves to love and serve God with an undivided heart.

Ordained Priesthood

Catholic priests are ordained into a special vocation called **Holy Orders**. Priests act "_in persona Christi_," which means "in the person of Christ." This means God works through priests to do the things that Jesus did on earth before

 **In Your Faith**

The simple difference between a religious sister and a nun is this: nuns commit their lives totally to prayer, separated from the world, while sisters commit their lives to deep prayer as well as going out into the world to perform service in many different ministries.

Notes and Nuggets

The "Five L's" are a framework of vocation formation for young people as articulated by the ministry of Dumb Ox Productions and briefly outlined on their website: www.DumbOxProductions.com. Used with permission.

He ascended to heaven. Like Jesus, Catholic priests commit their lives to the Church as their family. That is why priests are called "Father." They serve their family, the Church, in all the really meaningful times of life. They attend weddings and baptisms. They help people through the hard times of life like serious illness, divorce, or death. Through the power of the Holy Spirit, priests are God's special instruments who bring the sacraments to us. When they consecrate the bread and wine at Mass, the elements become the Body and Blood of Christ. When we go to confession, they absolve our sins.

Discernment and the Five L's

Sometimes you see posters or billboards that say things like "Is God calling you?" The answer is "Duh! Of course!" You can be sure that you have a vocation. The question is simply which vocation God is calling you to.

First, be not afraid! God will never call you to a vocation that makes you miserable. Second, don't stress about figuring it out. God usually calls us to a particular vocation gradually. You don't have to know today or even in high school or college. Your job is simple. Just learn to listen to God and have the courage to trust Him.

This process of understanding your vocation by listening to God is called **discernment**. The most important parts of discernment are finding time for silent prayer and striving daily to grow in virtue as you learn to love unselfishly. There are also five practical steps to help you become more aware of God's plan. We have nicknamed them the "Five L's."

LOOK for the face of Christ. Jesus came to show us who we really are, so we should start by looking for Him. This isn't like playing "Where's Waldo?" with a bearded guy wearing sandals. Looking for Christ means training our eyes—and the eyes of our hearts—to see the places where Jesus is present to us. The Eucharist is a perfect example. At first glance, it looks like bread and wine, but when we learn to look deeply, we see that it is actually Jesus. Jesus is also present in other places in a hidden way. Maybe you will see Jesus in someone who needs your help. Maybe you will see Jesus in volunteer work. The places where you find Jesus are the places you are called to be. Look for Jesus in your daily life and, when you see Him, follow.

LISTEN to the voice of Christ. In our crowded, noisy lives, it can be hard to listen to God because we can't hear Him in the first place! So we have to listen harder. This means taking time for prayer. First, reading the Bible is an important part of listening to Christ in prayer. If we don't know God's Word, how can we know what He is saying to us? In fact, St. Jerome said, "Ignorance of Scripture is ignorance of Christ." Pick a short Bible passage and ask Jesus what He wants to tell you through it. Then, sit quietly and read the passage slowly again. Be open to any particular words or phrases that strike you, and then relate your own ideas and feelings about them back

In Your Faith

"I will take my stand to watch, and station myself on the tower, and look forth to see what he will say to me." – Habakkuk 2:1

"We must understand that in order 'to do,' we must first learn 'to be,' that is to say, in the sweet company of Jesus in adoration." – Blessed Pope John Paul II

to God. If this sounds like a conversation, it is! Good times to do this are first thing in the morning or before you go to bed. Second, Eucharistic adoration is a powerful way to pray. Spend time with Jesus in the Eucharist, either near a tabernacle at church or in an adoration chapel. Instead of talking, just listen. Even just five or ten minutes will make a big difference. Third, listen to Jesus' voice when He speaks through others, especially those whom you know to be good examples of what it means to be a Christian.

LEARN your purpose. Learning is important, especially about the most important things in life! This program has focused a lot on your human identity and why God made you. Really try to learn these truths—not just memorize them. What is your real goal in life? It's not just to get an "A" on your report card or to be a world champion athlete, but to be fulfilled, happy, and with God. Learning to be holy and specifically striving to be with God as a young man or a young woman is where the learning sometimes gets tricky. But when you put this goal first, all your other goals will fall into place. Jesus made a promise about this. He said, "Seek first the kingdom of God and his righteousness, and all these things will be given you besides" (Matthew 6:33). He doesn't break promises. Another way to learn about your purpose is to visit a married couple, a convent, monastery, or seminary to get a real feel for how your gifts and desires may fit with the life of these people you visit.

LIVE it to the max. The Christian life is not supposed to be boring. It's an adventure. It's about living life to the maximum, not the minimum. There's an old Christian saying, "Remember your death." Sound spooky? Well, it could be, but when we remember that this world isn't permanent, we have two choices. We can either get scared or we can start making each day count. It doesn't mean living in fear. In fact, it's the opposite. It's like spiritual bungee jumping. You're nervous at the edge, but the rush that comes from living a proactive and confident life makes you want to leap again and again. Be proactive and confident about the life you live. You've probably already experienced the deep satisfaction that comes from doing something 100 percent—all the way. So, try it with your faith. Make your days count to the max. Do volunteer work, get more involved at your church, and try different things. Be virtuous. Be different. Be bold. Live your faith in courageous ways. As the old saying goes, "If you don't stand for something, you're going to fall for anything." Living your faith in a radical way brings great freedom and great joy, and it also brings confidence as you discern God's call in your life. This will help to make the next step as clear as it needs to be.

LOVE like God. This one is the most important. If you want to know your vocation, you need to practice loving like God loves. That means loving with your whole heart—selflessly. The more we love others, the more we become our true selves. When we focus on others before ourselves and live for God by loving like He loves, we finally fulfill who He made us to be. If you learn to love like God in your daily life, then discerning your vocation will become an exciting adventure, not a stressful experience.

These five steps will help you have better relationships and be happier and freer. When you need to know, God will make clear what your next step should be and give you the peace and courage to take that step. You will gradually see more and more where you are called—to marriage, consecrated life, or priesthood. You will also understand how to use your talents to serve God best.

Remember, you are unique and unrepeatable. God, who knows and loves you, has a unique and unrepeatable plan for your life.

IF YOU ASK ME ...

Three things that distract me from seeing Jesus' face and hearing God's voice:

1. _____
2. _____
3. _____

Three things I could do in order to see Jesus more clearly in my daily life and listen more closely to God's voice:

1. _____
2. _____
3. _____

In Your Faith

Mary is the Church's highest example of listening to God's plan and carrying it out. When God invited Mary to her own particular vocation, she said, "Behold, I am the handmaid of the Lord. May it be done to me according to your word" (Luke 1:38). What Mary told the servants at the wedding feast at Cana, later, is still the greatest advice of all: "Do whatever he tells you" (John 2:5). No one wants to help you get closer to Jesus more than His mother. Ask Mary for help living out the "Five L's"; she mastered all five in her own life! She is our Mother in heaven whose prayers will help you find your vocation.

What about Now?

One practical question you may ask is how to live out the "Five L's" in your everyday life. Sometimes advice about how to live our faith can seem hard to fit into our unique schedules and personalities. You can start by setting aside just five minutes of quiet prayer each day. Spending five minutes listening to God can make a big difference in how you spend the rest of the day.

You can also start spending quality time with your friends and family. Having fun with others can be an opportunity to look for the face of Jesus, to hear his voice, to learn, live, and love. Allow the "Five L's" to find their way into your daily habits. You may find it helpful to review your day each evening, asking yourself, *How did I or did I not look for the face of Christ, listen to His voice, etc.?* Reviewing your day takes only a few minutes and can be a prayerful way to fall asleep. *As you review, celebrate* with Jesus whatever you did faithfully and *resolve* to do better tomorrow in areas where you fell short. A good way to get better at anything is consistently reviewing and working on your goals.

Doing a daily review may reveal things in your routine that you should cut back or avoid entirely. Like what? Remember the activity at the beginning of

Notes and Nuggets:

If you choose "B" below, reserve the church or chapel beforehand. If this is not possible, try to dedicate part of the room as a prayer space with candles and a crucifix. Avoid having students who may distract each other sit together. Give the group ten to fifteen minutes for this exercise.

A. "Five L's" Poster

Have each student make a poster illustrating the "Five L's." You may want to provide poster board, markers, stickers, glue, magazines for clipping images, etc.

B. Prayer Time—*Lectio Divina*: **"Word of God"**

Before taking the students into the church, adoration chapel, or another suitable place of prayer, have them open their Bibles and select a familiar passage. Some suggestions: John 1:35-39; Mark 5:25-34; Matthew 17:1-8; Luke 11:9-13. Once everyone is ready, say "Imagine Jesus speaking to you in this passage. When He says something to the person (you), stop reading, put down the Bible, have a moment of silence, and ask yourself, 'How will I respond to Jesus? What do I want? What do I want to say to Him?' Next—and this is crucial—wait for Him to respond. He will."

VIDEO

Play "Man on the Street" and "Trivia" before Work It Out.

In Your Faith

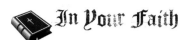

Paragraph 1877 in the Catechism says: "The vocation of humanity is to show forth the image of God and to be transformed into the image of the Father's only Son." This means that all of us are called to show the world who God is by becoming more like Jesus! Wow! How are we going to do that, except through love? St. Therese of Lisieux, a French saint who died in 1897 at age twenty-four, really captured this teaching in her simple motto: "My vocation is love!"

Closing Prayer

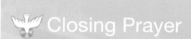

Let us thank God for the Good News we have heard in this chapter as we pray:

Blessed the people the Lord has chosen to be His own. From heaven the LORD looks down; He sees all mankind. Our soul waits for the LORD, who is our help and our shield.

May Your kindness, O LORD, be upon us who have put our hope in You.

Glory be to the Father and to the Son and to the Holy Spirit. As it was in the beginning, is now, and ever shall be, world without end. Amen.

– From Psalm 62

this chapter. Too much noise in our lives drowns out God's voice. If we live noisy lives, it is much harder to recognize God's voice and follow His lead. For example, as long as you watch uplifting shows, some TV is fine. But too much TV, too much Internet, obsessive texting, or any other kind of constant distraction can sidetrack us from our real purpose.

Maybe you also wonder about dating. Remember that the real purpose of dating is to find a spouse and discern the vocation of marriage. Practically speaking, this is often not the purpose that dating serves. Dating can be intense, confusing, dramatic, and even hurtful. These problems often come from speaking lies with the language of the body, but also from too much seriousness in relationships. These experiences can leave you confused, hurt, and not very hopeful about the future. Committing sexual sins will guarantee that your experience of middle school and high school is even more confusing and negatively dramatic. Chastity, on the other hand, will enable you to focus on the right things and become who God knows you can be. That's why it is best to spend time with a group of friends rather than deal with the pressure of exclusive (just the two of you) relationships. You will have plenty of time for exclusive relationships later. Why enter a serious relationship now when there is little chance of it lasting?

With your group of friends, practice the "Five L's" by treating others as brothers and sisters. Practice being kind, considerate, attentive, forgiving, and helpful. Also practice these attitudes with your parents and siblings, too. If you keep your relationships focused on these virtues you will have a much clearer and more hopeful vision of God's plan for you.

WORK IT OUT

A. Vocation Detective

Interview all three of the following: a married couple, a religious sister or brother, and a priest. Ask them about their experiences of their vocations. Ask each person the following four questions. Bring your interview next time to discuss their answers.

- How did you know you were called to be in your vocation?
- What does a typical day of your life look like?
- How is your vocation helping you get to heaven?
- How does your vocation help others get to heaven?

B. Five L's Rap/Song

Compose a rap or a song to help you remember the "Five L's." (You could always use the tune of a song that you already know.) Perform it if you dare!

Got It?

1. Holiness

2. 1. Marriage

   2. Consecrated Life

   3. Ordained Life

3. Look, Listen, Learn, Live, Love

GOT IT?

1. "_____is not a luxury for a few, but a simple duty for you and me." – Blessed Mother
   Teresa of Calcutta

2. Three vocations in the Church are...

   1._____2. _____3. _____

3. The Five L's are...

   L _____L _____L _____

   L _____L _____

VŌ·CAB'·U·LAR'·Ȳ

MARRIAGE:
A sacramental, holy bond, binding until death, between a man and a woman and God in which a couple becomes a sign of Christ and the Church. Marriage calls for a free, total, faithful, and fruitful relationship that brings new life into the world.

CONSECRATED LIFE:
A vocation in which a man or a woman vows to love God, often lived in a community of others with the same call. Consecrated religious men are often called "brothers" or "monks" while consecrated women are usually called "nuns" or "sisters."

HOLY ORDERS:
The sacrament received when a man enters *ordained life* by being ordained as a priest, deacon, or bishop. Men who receive Holy Orders in the Roman Catholic Church have a special responsibility to be God's instruments by giving the sacraments and being totally dedicated to the Church instead of to a wife and children.

DISCERNMENT:
The process of listening to God in order to understand gradually His particular calling for you, then choosing to respond "Yes."

VOCATION: First, the universal call to holiness that each of us received at our baptism. Next, this is the particular, specific way that God calls a person to live out their call to holiness in marriage, consecrated life, or ordained life.

Objectives:

This chapter strives to help middle schoolers do the following:

- Trust in God's plan for their futures
- Embrace their baptismal promises in a living relationship with Jesus Christ
- Use their bodies to "speak" the truth
- Apply core concepts of the Theology of the Body to the following:
  - Friends: bullying, gossip, peer pressure, social justice
  - Family: broken or dysfunctional families, lack of intimacy with parents, siblings
  - World: works of mercy, social justice
- Overcome fear and make a deeper commitment to embrace and live their Catholic faith

Notes and Nuggets:

The Theology of the Body has so many great applications beyond the framework for a chastity program. Therefore, this whole program reflects that range by being geared toward the overall formation of young Catholics. In this final chapter, we will explore applications of the Theology of the Body in everyday living and encourage middle schoolers to make a deep commitment to using the language of their bodies to "speak" only the truth of God's love.

Tune In:

Dare You to Move — Switchfoot, *Beautiful Letdown*

Come to Jesus — Josh Blakesley, *Waiting*

Lay It Down — Matt Maher, *Empty and Beautiful*

Waiting for No One — Mike Mangione, *Tenebrae*

Enough — Jeremy Camp, *The Carried Me Project*

From the Inside Out — Hillsong, *United We Stand*

Note: These songs are available online. Consider encouraging your students to find and download them.

Chapter Eight

Hope and Future
Daily Living Out the Language of the Body

Opening Prayer:

You can close this prayer with something like the following: "Lord, help us, through this chapter, to apply all that we have learned to our relationships with our friends and family. Help us commit our bodies and souls to live completely for you, embracing lives of real love, even when it is hard. Lord, help us to love you more purely each day of our lives until we are one day face to face with you in heaven. Amen."

Icebreaker

Fear of Commitment

This chapter is largely about overcoming our fear and trust issues in order to live out our commitment to Christ. This brief game helps illustrate that we have nothing to fear in following God. Have a volunteer come forward. Smile and ask, "Do you trust me?" Play up the question's intensity by asking it several times, even if the volunteer responds positively. After establishing that the volunteer trusts you, produce an official-looking paper contract that says, "I will do whatever (insert your name here) asks me to do next." Ask the volunteer to sign. He or she may do it right away or may hesitate. If necessary, ask for another volunteer. Then produce a paper bag. Ask again, "Do you trust me?" (By now there should be some suspicion about your motives.) Ask the volunteer to put his or her hand inside the paper bag without looking. Really try to emphasize the "fear of the unknown" factor. Once the volunteer trusts you and follows your instructions, he or she should find in the bag enough candy for everyone in the group. Instruct the volunteer to distribute the candy while you make a point about trust and fear.

VIDEO

Play "Introduction" and "Big Questions" before Story Starter.

Opening Prayer

Leader: In the name of the Father and of the Son and of the Holy Spirit *(all make the Sign of the Cross).*

All respond: In the divine image, Lord, You created him; male and female You created them.

Reader 1: God, You made us good, both body and soul.

Response: In the divine image, Lord, You created him; male and female You created them.

Reader 2: God, You saw that it was not good for us to be alone, so You gave us one another for loving relationships.

Response: In the divine image, Lord, You created him; male and female You created them.

Reader 3: God, You are love, and You made us for love.

Response: In the divine image, Lord, You created him; male and female You created them.

Reader 4: God, You made us without anything to hide from You.

Response: In the divine image, Lord, You created him; male and female You created them.

Reader 5: God, You made us to be happy with You forever.

Response: In the divine image, Lord, You created him; male and female You created them.

Leader: Jesus, You taught us to address Your Father as You did, and so in the Holy Spirit we pray…

All: Our Father…

notes

 **STORY STARTER**

Carded

The first time I ever attended a Catholic youth conference, one of the main talks was about sex, chastity, and commitment. I was thirteen. Honestly, I can't even remember the speaker's name, but I do remember feeling absolutely convinced that her basic message was true: sexual activity should be saved for marriage. Her words convicted me to trust God's plan for my life and wait for my future spouse.

At the end of the talk, ushers walked up and down the aisles to pass out chastity pledge cards. The cards read: "Believing that sex is a gift reserved for marriage, I commit to save myself for my future spouse." There was a

spot to sign and date the card. I knew making the commitment and signing the card was the right thing to do, that I would never regret making the pledge. But I also knew that it would be difficult to keep this promise. With a prayer, I signed the card and, from that day on, took my commitment very seriously.

Eleven years later, my wife and I sat in our living room as she went through an old box of mementos—notes, cards, clippings, and pictures—from high school. From the pile, she pulled out a card that looked familiar. Actually, it looked *very* familiar—in fact, it was exactly like the chastity pledge card that I had signed so many years before.

Her signature and the date on which she had signed it were at the bottom. As I looked at it, I was amazed. The date on her card was the same date that I had signed mine eleven years earlier. We realized we had both been at the same conference! The amazing thing is that I grew up in Rhode Island, while she was from Louisiana. *Two people who would not even meet for another nine years made a commitment to each other at the same time in the same place without even knowing it.* We were loving each other even before we met.

Neither my wife nor I knew what God had planned for our future. We just knew that it was best to trust that His way was the best way. Even though it would be years before we saw the reward of committing to God's way, God knew exactly what He was doing. He had already planned every detail.

That day in our living room as Aimee and I shared our chastity pledged cards, we realized once again the most important truth of all: Living God's plan for love simply means trusting God and allowing Him to give us the blessings He has planned for us from the beginning of time itself.

—Colin MacIver

BRIDGING THE  GAP

Making a commitment to do things God's way is a big step but one that makes perfect sense. When we remember what He has done for us, we remember that God is already totally committed to us. Our "yes" just gives Him the opportunity to give us what is best for us.

Knowing God's way and growing in the necessary grace to live it out take a lifetime of courage and commitment. Once we commit to living God's way, we have to grow toward our goal every day. If you wanted to take a road trip to Disney World, you couldn't get there just by sitting in the parked car in the driveway. You would actually have to move toward your destination little by little.

Remember that chastity, for example, is not just abstinence. Saving the full gift of your sexuality for your spouse doesn't just mean not having sex. Chastity means that we live lives of purity. In other words, you don't do anything that you would not want some other person doing with your future husband or wife. It also means practicing unselfish love for others, saying yes to the help that Jesus offers you, and learning to speak the truth with the language of your body.

The Theology of the Body helps us learn the true language of our bodies. Our souls are happy and healthy when we learn to say with the language of our bodies what is actually true about our relationships. Saying "no" to sex outside of marriage is a part of speaking truthfully with the language of our bodies. But growing in the virtues and receiving grace through the sacraments also makes us more fluent in saying "yes" through our language of the body as God intended it.

IF YOU ASK ME ...

1. List three people or organizations you've made a commitment to:

_____

_____

_____

2. I'm glad I made a commitment to _____ because _____. I thought that _____ was really easy, but then I discovered that it took _____.

TO THE CORE

Have you ever thought about your faith as a part of your body? Because the spiritual world is invisible, sometimes we tend to separate our faith as something only mental, not physical. Yet think about how often our Catholic faith refers to the body and the body's language. The Eucharist is not bread but the Body of Christ. The Church is not a building with a steeple and pews but the Body of Christ. Jesus, who "spoke" His love for us through the language of His body on the Cross, continues to "speak" His love for us through the language of His body in the Church.

The sacraments especially show how important the language of the body is in the Church. When you receive a sacrament, something happens with your body that reveals what God is doing in your soul. Think about your

Notes and Nuggets:

You can use the questions in this paragraph as starters for a short discussion with your group about putting faith into action—responding to God's love not only in concept but in real choices expressed through the body. You are likely to get examples like "praying," "going to Mass," etc., but try to move the discussion beyond expected responses to less conventional examples. Suggest that responding to God's love happens in ordinary moments throughout the day.

baptism, for example. Water was poured over your body as a visible sign that the grace of the sacrament was cleansing your soul and allowing you to become a true child of God. Later, every time you participate in Mass, you renew your relationship with God that started at baptism. Genuflecting, making the Sign of the Cross, standing for the Gospel reading, and kneeling during the prayers of consecration show that your body is speaking a language that reveals your relationship with and worship of God. When you receive Communion, your body—and therefore all of you—is united with Jesus in the Eucharist. When blessed oil is traced onto your forehead at confirmation, your soul is sealed with the power to live and share your faith.

The sacraments are the visible ways that God expresses the invisible reality of His love in our lives. He does this through the language of the human body: words and signs that we can experience. Since the sacraments flow from Christ and they flow only through the Church, it is through the Church that God tells us He is totally committed to our happiness and salvation. Then He invites us to respond to His love and return His commitment.

But what does it mean to respond to God's love? How do you use the language of your body in everyday life to return God's commitment? What can you do today to grow in your commitment to Him and His plan for your life?

True Friendship Speaks the Truth

You can also practice speaking the truth with the language of your body through practicing true friendship. True friends are like teammates on a gold-medal team. Good teammates challenge and support each other. They express their commitment to each other by practicing hard together. They strive to improve each other's skills. During a tough game, they encourage each other to play hard and keep going. They applaud each other's achievements, they encourage each other when things go wrong, and they eventually win—by working together.

We should support our friends even more in the most important game—life. True friends help each other become the best people they can be, even when it's tough. They challenge and support each other toward the goal of practicing virtue. They encourage each other in weak moments.

This is much different—and better—than the back-stabbing and drama that often happens among people your age. We have all seen "friendships" that are held together by nothing more than destructive, negative actions like bullying, gossiping, texting instead of listening, drinking, disobeying parents, or partying. These "friendships" tear down instead of build up.

Bad peer pressure makes it hard to break free from destructive, false "friendship." Sometimes bad peer pressure is hard to recognize. When

Notes and Nuggets:

Here are a few questions to help middle schoolers reflect on the value of being a true friend:

Name some characteristics of a true friend. Are these the things that most middle schoolers are searching for when trying to fit into certain groups? If not, why not? Are you a good friend? If one of your friends was interviewed, what would be a weakness they may mention about you being a friend? What would they say are your strong points of being a good friend? What can we learn from Christ about being a good friend?

Notes and Nuggets:

Bullying remains a major issue in the lives of many middle schoolers. "Cyber bullying" is an ongoing, hostile affront by one child toward another using interactive technologies. This type of bullying, done mostly through the Internet and cell phones, is an increasingly common method of intimidation or harassment. For this technology-savvy generation, these media have made it easier to bully someone without getting caught. The use of temporary email addresses and other ways of remaining anonymous can make it difficult to track down a cyber bully. Cyber bullying takes various forms: texting threatening messages; posting online derogatory comments or pictures; spreading rumors in massive electronic form; hacking into someone else's social networking profile to falsely attribute out-of-character or troublesome comments; stealing passwords to exploit personal email accounts; sexually harassing another via instant messages; and other forms. Even a small "joke" in the cyber world can quickly become a means of wounding and even paralyzing the victim with vicious psychological "games" that cause major problems. The numerous ways to hurt another via electronic media are truly astounding, and ours is only a very short list.

It is appropriate to address this issue as part of a group discussion about respect for others, emphasizing that just as social communication devices can bring great good and bring people together, they can also be misused to great harm. The fact that much of this interaction is "invisible" to adults increases the volume of potential bullying because physical presence is no longer required. Even one embarrassing or maliciously altered photo posted online may follow a middle schooler for years. The basic point to emphasize is that respect for the human person must be expressed through the language of the body at all times, even when we are using technology with our bodies.

Asking your group to name some of the ways that they see people disrespecting others with technology could produce an array of topics that goes beyond cyber bullying, but remind your students that there is only one world in which we live. Whether we are acting in the "virtual" world or "real" world, we are always interacting with real persons who have real hearts and real minds. Friends don't let friends bully others. Period. Help them remain aware of the dangers by applying the Golden Rule to digital activity: Am I doing unto others through technology as I would have them do unto me?

someone says that something wrong is "so cool," you may not vocally disagree because you're afraid of not being "cool." Sometimes nobody even says anything out loud, but you join in something destructive because it seems like everyone around you is doing it, too.

But is that what you really want in your friendships? Pressure, teasing, or bullying? Wouldn't your true friends try to help you become a more, instead of a less, virtuous person? And what do you really want to give your friends in return? Are you just looking for company in your bad habits, or do you want to help them become their best?

Speak the truth with the language of your body in friendship. Be a true friend! Instead of dragging down others into bad habits, treat them with respect. Instead of making fun of them, honor people who have refused to give in to bad peer pressure. Remember that no matter how popular or unpopular someone is, everyone has the enormous dignity of being made in God's own image and likeness.

Family Love Speaks the Truth

Have you ever noticed that sometimes family members treat each other worse than they treat total strangers? And our families are usually the people whom we love most!

Why do you think this happens?

The family is so important to our growth in faith that it even has its own commandment: "Honor your mother and your father." The family is like a little Church, sometimes called "the domestic Church." In this little Church, parents and children are called to use the language of their bodies to be visible signs of God's unconditional love. By remaining committed to each other through good and bad times, family members can reflect God's eternal commitment to us. By loving and sacrificing for each other in bodily choices, family members can reflect to each other God's unconditional love. For example, you can do this by listening to your sister talk about her hard day, playing with your little brother instead of staying in your room, helping your mom make dinner, and asking your dad about his work. All these things reflect God's concern for every aspect of our lives.

At the same time, you know all too well that your parents, brothers, and sisters aren't perfect. Many families experience struggles. Many families go through tough times. Many families argue or even sometimes say hurtful things. Because you're so aware of your family's flaws, it can be easy to lose your patience or get annoyed with your parents or siblings. Sometimes it can take even more practice to love your family than it does to love anyone else! Even Blessed Mother Teresa understood this when she said, "Sometimes it

is harder for us to smile at those who live with us, the immediate members of our family, than it is to smile at those who are not that close to us."

Some families deal with even tougher issues, such as job loss, serious illnesses, divorce, or death. But no matter what hurts or problems a family may experience, God loves each family member and wants to heal any wounds. Even if our families let us down, the love of God the Father for us, His children, makes us part of an eternal family that is so safe and stable that nothing can break it apart.

Expressing love for your family through the language of your body is powerful. Whenever you help your parents around the house, speak kindly to your siblings, apologize for your mistakes, and forgive the mistakes of others, you are speaking love and commitment through your actions. And that means you have the power to help your family understand and experience the even greater love and commitment of God. Being a visible sign of God's love in the family may sometimes begin with you.

Chastity Speaks the Truth

Chastity is the virtue that allows us to speak the truth with the language of our bodies. Chastity gives our bodies the ability to speak love and commitment in the way that matches the truth of our relationships. To practice chastity, we must pay attention to the modesty of our clothing, choose wholesome entertainment (TV, movies, music, and games), and speak with respect and purity. Whatever we text, email, and post online must build up others and never treat them like objects. Chastity flows not just from a checklist of do's and don't's but from the heart.

One way to commit to chastity is praying for your future vocation today. Whether you enter marriage, priesthood, or consecrated life, you can pray now for the people you will be called to love and serve one day. Remembering that people connected to your future vocation will be affected by your choices today can help you choose wisely.

Helping Others Speaks the Truth

We will discuss one last way to speak truthfully with the language of your body—helping people who are poor or outcast from society. Think about what Jesus did during His earthly ministry. He spent most of His time with people who had serious needs. He healed people who were blind, crippled, and diseased. He accepted people who were rejected and mistreated by others. He listened to people who felt left out and hopeless.

We should imitate Jesus by doing what we can in our own situations to help others. Maybe you can't heal someone's blindness, but you could invite someone who looks lonely to sit with you at lunch. You could volunteer at a food bank, visit a nursing home, or participate in programs at your parish.

In Your Faith

Sometimes you may wonder if you really have what it takes to figure out your future on your own. But as you begin training for your specific vocation, remember your life is an adventure you share with your friends and family. As John Paul II reminded us, "You must never think that you are alone in deciding your future! And second: when deciding your future, you must not decide for yourself alone!" In other words, your vocational decision affects the Body of Christ; it is not only for your happiness but the happiness of many.

Notes and Nuggets:

Consider taking some time to help your middle schoolers reflect on the power that fear can have in our lives if not submitted to God and overcome by His love. Pass around a hat and have each of them write three fears that they experience or see in their peers (without naming the peers) and collect them in the hat. Compile the responses anonymously on a whiteboard or poster board, checkmarking the fears that come up more than once. If a particular response seems to stand out, note to the group that they are not alone in their fears. (You may choose to leave any inappropriate or sarcastic responses off the list.) Afterward, lead a group discussion to identify the effects of each fear in our lives. Finally, help them to see how God can help overcome each fear with the security of His faithful love.

Blessed Teresa of Calcutta reminds us of the importance of a daily relationship with Jesus. She advises that looking and listening—two of the Five L's we reviewed in the last chapter— truly lead us to recognize and love Christ in the poor: "I worry some of you still have not really met Jesus—one to one—you and Jesus alone. We may spend time in chapel, but have you seen with the eyes of your soul how he looks at you with love? Do you really know the living Jesus, not from books, but from being with him in your heart? Have you heard the loving words he speaks to you? ... Until you can hear Jesus in the silence of your own heart, you will not be able to hear him saying 'I thirst' in the hearts of the poor. Never give up this daily intimate contact with Jesus as the real living person—not just the idea ... Our soul needs that as much as the body needs to breathe the air."

"There is no fear in love, but perfect love casts out fear." – 1 John 4:18

The Church teaches us the Corporal (Bodily) Works of Mercy, which show the love of Christ to others through the language of the body: feed the hungry, give drink to the thirsty, shelter the homeless, care for the sick, visit the imprisoned, clothe the naked, and bury the dead.

By serving others, you won't just help them—you will also grow in your relationship with Jesus. And you will allow God to speak to others through your gift of self through the language of your body. Who knows what wonderful things God can do and say through you if you are open?

Be Not Afraid

If you had to guess, what do you think is the number one, most repeated idea in the New Testament? You may be surprised to learn that it is "be not afraid." In fact, the message not to fear is even repeated more than the message to love.

Why? If fear is such a constant theme, it must be a very common problem. Christ does not want fear to rule our lives. He wants *love* to rule our lives! The Good News is that "there is no fear in love, but perfect love casts out fear" (1 John 4:18). So overcoming fear must be an important step to real, self-giving love. Think about all the ways fear prevents us from doing things God's way—the best way. We are afraid that we will fail a test, so we are tempted to cheat. Not God's way. We are afraid that people will make fun of us, so we are tempted to participate in gossip. Not God's way. We are afraid that nobody likes us, so we are tempted to use our bodies to attract attention. Not God's way.

The most destructive fear of all is being afraid of what will happen if we commit our lives to God. The world's rewards are loud, in our faces, and seem to offer instant gratification. The rewards of following God, however, often require us to sacrifice and put others first. Sometimes we might fear that if we follow God's way, we will miss out on all the fun and excitement.

But being afraid of God is like being afraid of Santa Claus. God wants to give you only good things. He's the president of your fan club. God's greatest desire is for you to experience true happiness and love through a relationship with Him. And only God can empower you to love yourself and others with real love so you can experience real fulfillment during your life now and, ultimately, forever in heaven.

Both Blessed John Paul II and Pope Benedict XVI called the whole Church to confront fear during their first days as pope. Yet both knew that fear is just a waste of time and energy, so they rejected fear and turned to God's love. Some of John Paul's first words as pope were "Be not afraid!" In Pope Benedict's first homily as pope, he quoted words that John Paul II had said many years before: "If we let Christ into our lives, we lose nothing, nothing,

APPLICATION

COMMITMENT

Invite middle schoolers to make a commitment to God, others, and themselves through chastity. You can use the following format for a special prayer service to conclude the program. This prayer service incorporates what the *Catechism*, when speaking about chastity, calls the "laws of growth." The middle schoolers are being invited to make a commitment to grow intentionally toward this virtue. The process is more developed than signing an abstinence pledge, because this commitment is to practice a virtue actively and not just passively avoid a behavior.

You can make the prayer both meaningful and memorable in several special ways. You may hold it in a church or chapel. You may invite a priest or deacon to preside. We recommend, if possible, changing the venue from your normal meeting place in order to help signify the special nature of this moment. If you hold it as a simple prayer service in your classroom or regular meeting place, consider changing the environment a bit or incorporating some candles and music. In any format, it is a great opportunity to manifest the idea of commitment and to pray for your young people to answer St. Paul's calling: "Be blameless and innocent, children of God without blemish in the midst of a crooked and perverse generation, among whom you shine like lights in the world" (Philippians 2:15).

absolutely nothing of what makes life free, beautiful and great. No! Only in this friendship are the doors of life opened wide. Only in this friendship is the great potential of human existence truly revealed. Only in this friendship do we experience beauty and liberation" (Homily in St. Peter's Square, April 24, 2005).

This is the promise of Jesus Himself, too. In John 10:10, Jesus said, "I came that they may have life and have it abundantly." Do you know what *abundant* actually means? When you have something abundantly, you have *more* than enough. *Abundant* means way above and beyond the minimum.

Think about how Jesus' whole life is full of abundance. For example, when He multiplied the fishes and loaves for a hungry crowd, people did not just have enough to tide them over until dinner. Everybody—several thousand people—ate until they were full, and then there were still twelve whole baskets of food left over. Jesus provided abundantly for their needs—more than they could ever expect.

No matter who has disappointed you in your life, Jesus will always keep His promises and exceed your hopes and dreams. After all, you can trust Someone who died for you.

Are you ready for the adventure of following Him?

IF YOU ASK ME ...

1. I used to be afraid of _____ but now I'm not.

2. I want to conquer my fear of _____.

Notes and Nuggets:

Invite students to come forward one-by-one to sign their names to the pledge. You might also want to give each middle schooler his or her own personal commitment card. These are found at chastity.com. Whether they all sign the document or each receive a card, it is best to stress that this is an invitation and that no one will be forced to sign. This is a personal commitment. It adds to the atmosphere if a kneeler is provided, placed in front of the Blessed Sacrament, preferably the monstrance, with a small table with a nice pen, so they sign there.

Gift Option: If you choose to give your middle schoolers a gift or take-home resource of some sort as you finish the program, this moment can serve as a good opportunity to give them such a gift.

VIDEO
Play "Closing" and "Trivia" before Work It Out.

Commitment

Sign of the Cross

Reading: Romans 12:1-2

I urge you therefore, brothers, by the mercies of God, to offer your bodies as a living sacrifice, holy and pleasing to God, your spiritual worship. Do not conform yourselves to this age but be transformed by the renewal of your mind, that you may discern what is the will of God, what is good and pleasing and perfect.

Read the pledge together:

- I promise, with the help of God's grace, to live my baptismal call through a commitment to chastity.

- I promise, with the help of God's grace, to learn to speak the truth through the language of my body.

- I reject the false promises of the world, and I trust in God's plan for me and my future.

- I pledge to strive for purity in the way that I live.

- I pledge to seek forgiveness, strength, and healing in the sacraments.

- I want to receive all that God has in store for me. Amen.

Closing Prayer:

Lord Jesus,

In your Cross and Resurrection, You showed us the power of the body to express true love.

Help us, Your disciples, to offer our bodies as signs of real love and commitment.

Protect us from impurity, hurt, and hopelessness and help us to receive your gift of selfless love.

In Your name we pray, Jesus Christ our Lord. Amen.

Notes and Nuggets:

You may want to combine these two activities and have your middle schoolers seal both their learning list and their letters in the envelope. Hold on to the letters for a few years (until they are at least sophomores in high school) and mail them when least expected. This creates a personalized time capsule for each student that will undoubtedly make quite an impact on his or her future self. Their more innocent, middle-school selves can remind their later high school selves of some very powerful truths in the future.

In directing "digital natives" in this activity: Don't be surprised if your middle schoolers don't know how to write a letter or address an envelope. It is a good idea to write a sample letter and instructions for addressing an envelope on the board and walk around to make sure that each person does this correctly. (If you want to save time, collect the letters and address them yourself at a later time.)

Got It?

1. Theology of the Body

2. sacraments

WORK IT OUT

A. Top Five + Five List

Write a list of five things that you learned in this program that you really want to remember. Then, for each of your top five things to remember, list one way that you can try to do more than remember—to *live out*—each of the five things you want to remember.

B. Dear Me...

Write a letter to your future self. Encourage yourself to stay true to your commitment and to live a pure and holy life according to the language of your body. Your leader will help you address the envelope where you will place your letter.

Closing Prayer

Let us thank God for the Good News we have heard in this chapter as we pray:

Only goodness and kindness follow me all the days of my life; and I shall dwell in the house of the LORD for years to come.

Glory be to the Father and to the Son and to the Holy Spirit. As it was in the beginning, is now, and ever shall be, world without end. Amen.

– From Psalm 23

GOT IT?

1. The _____ is about learning the true language of our bodies.   2

2. The_____ especially show how important the language of the body is in the Church.   2

Appendices

Appendix #1: Find Me Bingo

_____ has a birthmark

_____ speaks more than one language

_____ likes to eat veggies

_____ plays a musical instrument

_____ can imitate a Muppet

_____ is left-handed

_____ loves to play sports

_____ can do a trick with a yo-yo

_____ knows how to juggle

_____ has a quarter in their pocket or purse

_____ has a stay-at-home Mom

_____ likes country music

_____ has some Irish or Italian in their family

_____ owns a wooden baseball bat

_____ can speak another language fluently

_____ has a Facebook account

_____ has visited a nursing home, hospital, or served the poor in the past year

_____ has been to a foreign country

_____ can build or fix computers

_____ has a song more than twenty years old on their iPod or phone

_____ likes to go fishing or hunting

_____ has a relative who is a seminarian, priest, or religious

_____ has played a video game for more than four hours straight

_____ would rather hike in the mountains than go to the beach

_____ has seen the movie _The Passion of the Christ_

Notes and Nuggets:

The following case studies are designed to help your middle schoolers apply what they have learned to real life. They are designed to be a bit open-ended, and the analysis of the following scenarios will tell you quite a bit about the experiences of your middle schoolers so far. We have certain issues in mind for each of these, but others may surface as well. In writing this text, we heard from many of you about particular issues in your parishes and communities. This is to help you address them at the level and depth that is best for your particular group. Case studies, therefore, are not included in the Student Workbook.

It may be helpful to use a small group format for these, but we strongly recommend that each group have an experienced facilitator to guide the discussion.

Notes and Nuggets: Case Study #1

Case Study #1 helps begin the difficult discussion about how to handle the feelings of attraction middle schoolers inevitably experience. Minor, brief romances constantly emerge in middle school as students naturally develop. Your task here is to get your group to think about the healthiest and most age-appropriate ways to deal with these feelings.

Open their eyes to the benefit and necessity of simple male-female friendships. You might say to your group, "Even in the midst of attraction, it's more loving to keep things simple. Friendship is the foundation of any lasting love, so if you really like another person, the best thing is to enjoy being their friend without getting involved in the drama of a relationship."

Appendices

Appendix #2: Case Studies

CASE STUDY #1

Ben met Amanda three months ago at camp. They were both going into seventh grade and had many things in common. They were in many of the same activities. Both played soccer during the school year and listened to the same kind of music. During that week, Ben decided that he really liked being around Amanda. He really, really liked being around her. His friend Pete and some of his other friends noticed how Ben turned red when he was around Amanda, how he acted differently, and how he talked about her all the time:

Pete: "You like Amanda!"

Ben: "No, I don't. No way."

Pete: "Yes, you do. You want to kiss her. Ha! Ha! Ha! You should tell her!"

Ben: "Yeah?"

Pete: "Well, if you don't, I'm going to tell her."

So Ben decided to tell Amanda that he liked her. He didn't know exactly how to proceed, so he asked Pete, who told him that he should just text her—right now! Ben's hands got sweaty.

Ben: "Right now? What do I say?"

Pete: "Just say that you like her and ask her to be your girlfriend."

Ben thought for a second. He knew that there was nothing wrong with the way that he felt about her, but he also knew that she lived in New Jersey and he lived in Kentucky. He also knew that they were twelve years old and that neither was really ready to date—plus something about saying something important in a text seemed weird.

- What do you think?

- What are the problems in this situation?

- Is Pete helpful?

- Why did Ben want to talk to Amanda face-to-face instead of texting her?

- What would be the best way for Ben to deal with his feelings?

Notes and Nuggets: Case Study #2

Be sure to discuss the importance of avoiding bad situations or the near occasion of sin. Amber should certainly not go to Dave's house without supervision. Even if his intentions are honorable, the situation is likely to be a tempting opportunity for sexual activity. Emphasize that the situation itself is dangerous for the two of them because it creates temptation.

CASE STUDY #2

Amber had a serious crush on Dave. He sat next to her in math class and was always really nice to her. Amber talked about him to her friends all the time. One day, even though Amber had asked her not to, her friend Laurie told Dave that Amber liked him. Dave didn't really say anything, but the next day in math class, he gave Amber his phone number and she gave him hers. Amber was really excited when, after school, Dave sent her a text: "I like you too." She showed her friends, and they all squeaked with excitement. She texted Dave back: "Wanna do something this weekend?" He texted back immediately: "Want to come to my house on Saturday? My mom and dad are going out and only my big brother will be home."

- Why not just go out with a bunch of friends?

- Why do you think Dave texted Amber instead of talking to her?

- What should Amber do?

- What other activities might Amber suggest to Dave for the weekend?

CASE STUDY #3

Anna and Troy are in eighth grade and have been "going out" for a month. Her parents don't want Anna to date until she is a junior in high school so her relationship with Troy is a secret. Troy's parents don't pay nearly as much attention. Even though they are unaware that Troy and Anna are dating, they probably wouldn't really mind. Troy has had two other girlfriends, and those relationships lasted about two months each. He doesn't talk to either one anymore. Like Anna, the other two girls go to a different school than Troy. Anna met Troy at the mall one weekend at a mini-golf course where he and his friends tend to hang out on weekends. The mini-golf place is pretty popular. It is dark with black lit (glow-in-the-dark) attractions and loud music. It is also spread out so there are lots of places where you can hang out without any adult intervention. (Anna wasn't supposed to be there in the first place.) One night, Anna tells her parents that she is going to the mall with her friends, when in reality she is secretly meeting Troy to be alone with him. When they get to the mall, Anna's parents ask where her other friends are, and she explains that they must be the first ones there. So Anna's parents reluctantly drop her off with Anna's assurances that her friends are five minutes away. When Anna gets inside the mall Troy is there waiting in front of Old Navy. He and Anna go up to the mini-golf course next to the mall.

- What's wrong with this picture?

- What is so suspect about the mini-golf place?

Notes and Nuggets: Case Study #4

In recent years, some communities are discovering (and struggling with) middle school sexual experimentation rings taking place in public places like movie theaters. Thankfully, this may not be a feature of your community. On the other hand, it very well may be. Either way, this case study may help to surface things that are going on in the local weekend scene of your students. Your middle schoolers might speculate that there is drug use or drinking in the back of the movie theater, and, naturally, it would be helpful for them to avoid that. It may also become clear that other things—which may even require action on your part—are taking place in your town.

Notes and Nuggets: Case Study #5

This is another phenomenon we all wish were non-existent, but sexting or inappropriate sexual pictures sent through cell phones has become a real middle school problem. It is dangerous, dehumanizing, and abusive. The damaging effects are long lasting. If a particular instance surfaces here, be sure to talk to your D.R.E., principal, or pastor. Remind your students that any images sent over the phone or Internet become public property, and they will never be able to get them back. So if they send immodest images of themselves to a boyfriend or girlfriend, and the relationship ends, they will never know where the pictures may end up.

- List three things that Anna does wrong.

- Why might Anna be in some danger?

- Any problems with Troy's track record? Why or why not?

- If you were friends with Anna, what suggestions might you give her?

CASE STUDY #4

The movie theater is where everyone ends up on Friday night after football season is over. Parents figure that it is safe and contained and that there is a definite activity to keep their kids out of trouble. Joe and his friends go every weekend, whether there is something good to see or not. They have noticed that there is a group of kids in the grade ahead of them that hang out in the back of every movie. They know something strange is going on back there but aren't quite sure what. Joe asked his brother, who is a junior in high school, what happened back there, and his brother just told Joe to stay away. When Joe and his friends walk into a movie one weekend, they see their slightly older peers in the back, some guys and lots of girls. Joe realizes that he knows a few of the girls from school and says "hi" when they signal for him to come sit with them.

- Why is going to sit with them a bad idea?

- Why is Joe likely to sit there anyway?

- What could a good leader in Joe's group of friends do to help look out for everyone?

CASE STUDY #5

A group of girls sits at lunch on a Friday afternoon. Jamie looks across the cafeteria at a table full of guys where Leland and his friends are blowing spit balls at each other. Samantha: "Jamie, what's wrong?" Jamie hesitates, takes a bite of cafeteria peas, and shrugs, "Nothing." Samantha is a good friend and knows that nothing is code for everything. "Is it Leland?" Samantha knows that Jamie really likes him and that they have been talking. Jamie pulls out her cell phone and hands it to Samantha, who follows the text stream:

Leland: I don't think you really like me.

Jamie: What? LOL

Leland: I'm serious.

Jamie: What? Why not? What do you mean?

Leland: You won't prove it. My old girlfriend proved it.

Notes and Nuggets: Case Study #7

This is also an all-too-common scenario. Some parents are well aware of the dangers of unrestricted Internet access and the limitless supply of pornography that is available to middle schoolers. Many parents have taken appropriate precautions in their homes through protective software and supervised computer times. Others, who are less aware of the dangers, have had their precautions bypassed by open wireless networks in the neighborhood or other homes where there is less protection. (We have included help for parents in this regard in the *Theology of the Body for Teens: Middle School Edition* Parents Guide.)

Jamie: What do you mean?

Leland: If you really like me send me a pic of you that you wouldn't show anyone else.

Jamie: What? Are you serious?

Leland: Yes. If you really like me show me.

Jamie: ....

Samantha asked Jamie, "You didn't send him anything did you?" "Not yet," Jamie replied.

- What should Samantha say next?

- What are five reasons that Jamie should not send Leland a picture?

- Do guys as lost as Leland exist?

- Why would Jamie even consider this? What is she really looking for?

CASE STUDY #6

Mike is hanging out after practice with his teammates. His friend Sam asks him what he is doing later that night, when Mike says, "Going bowling with Bill, Molly, Brittney, and Steve." Sam's immediate response: "Molly is so hot! She's got a good body. Can I come?" Mike is taken aback a bit. Molly has been his friend since kindergarten. "Do you like her?" he asks. Sam: "Not really. She's just hot!"

- What should Mike's next line be?

- What is wrong with Sam's way of talking about Molly?

- Should Molly be flattered or a bit offended?

- Why might she be flattered anyway?

- Why might Mike just agree and stay quiet? Why is that such a problem?

CASE STUDY #7

Jerry's parents get him his first computer. He is really excited, and he already knows how to use it, probably ten times better than his parents. Jerry has all sorts of ideas. He talked his parents into getting Wi-Fi so that he can use it anywhere in the whole house. His parents don't know that much about computers and didn't really give him any warnings or restrictions other than "Make sure you use it. It cost a lot of money!" That won't be a problem for Jerry. Jerry immediately sets his own desktop

Notes and Nuggets: Case Study #8

This is a sort of "middle schooler retelling" of the story of a bishop and a harlot. In their story, two bishops see a prostitute and have two different responses. One looks away to avoid temptation, while the other sees her real beauty and the tragedy of her being used for her body. The bishop then ministers to her and so moves her heart that she becomes a saint. This case study should help your students to understand that chastity sees the whole person. While Nick is not sinning, and he is doing what he needs to do to avoid lustful thinking by having custody of his eyes—he still has some growing to do. Wade, on the other hand, shows self-mastery and a balanced sense of sexuality. He notices the girls' beauty, but he does not objectify or lust after them.

Notes and Nuggets: Case Study #9

This should spark some discussion on the "two-way street" of the self-image we present and how we are seen by others. John Paul II distinguishes the *ethos of the image* and the *ethos of seeing* (see TOB 63:6-7). He does this to speak about the distinction between art and pornography, but there is a very real application to modesty and self-presentation here, too. The ethos of the image refers to how a person is presented and what response is being evoked. We bear a moral responsibility for how we present ourselves, especially when we dress in such a way that might provoke lust. On the other hand, the ethos of seeing is about the moral responsibility of the one who views. Even if a person is presented to us with the purpose of evoking lust, we have the responsibility to take custody of our eyes and be disciplined in our thoughts.

Another important discussion here is about what the girls hope to get here: attention. Certainly they do not get the type of attention they are hoping for. Their deeper desire is to be seen as beautiful and lovable. Instead they get a counterfeit. They are seen as desirable and consumable. This is a very common phenomenon.

picture, opens his own Facebook account, sets up iTunes, starts gaming with his friends, and spends hours every night on the computer.

- What apparent problems will Jerry run into?

- With all of that technology at his fingertips, what might Jerry miss out on?

- Why might it be dangerous for Jerry to have unfiltered Internet access anywhere he wants?

- If you were computer safety experts, what would you tell Jerry's parents?

CASE STUDY #8

Three friends, Nick, Kevin, and Wade, are hanging out on a weekend. A group of girls walks by. Each of the guys notices them and responds differently.

Nick looks down, then tells the other guys to cover their eyes so that they don't sin. Kevin looks up and down at them and tells the other two how good- looking they are. Wade sees them, notices that they are pretty, and makes a comment that the girl in the middle looks a lot like a girl at school. Then he asks the other guys if they want to go play video games.

- Which responses from the three boys present a problem?

- Why is Nick's response often a very good one?

- Which response shows the most mature understanding of the truth of the human body?

CASE STUDY #9

Three girls go out on a Friday night to their parish festival. They all get dressed up like they are going out to a club. They are dressed immodestly and are hoping to be noticed. Walking around at the festival, a group of guys whom they don't know is noticeably staring. The girls notice being noticed, whisper, and giggle to each other. The guys start to call out and make loud, rude comments. The girls go from being flattered to feeling uncomfortable.

- Whose fault is this?

- What could the girls have done to avoid this situation?

- How about the guys (more obvious here)?

- Why did the girls dress that way in the first place?

Appendices

Appendix #3: Leader's Notes for Chapter 6

I've heard that Catholics should have as many kids as possible. Is that true?

Only God knows the hearts of couples who contracept; often, they do not know the truth of their actions. Yet because Jesus said, "The truth will set you free," we have included these responses to help prevent people from experiencing the pain of doing wrong, even unwittingly. This is one reason the Theology of the Body is so timely—it will help heal our misled culture.

Sex is meant to reflect God's love. God's love gives life. As a sign, sex should reflect this life-giving characteristic. Sadly, our culture rejects this dimension of sex by widespread use of contraception. Contraception includes any method that intentionally blocks the possibility of new life that is intrinsic to sex: condoms, birth control pills, patches, implants, male withdrawal, or any other device or behavior that alters sex with the intention of preventing new life. In this way, contraception destroys a major way that sex can remind us of God's love.

Contracepting couples also hold back part of themselves from each other, which diminishes the totality of their self-gift. Contraceptive sex says, "I give you all of myself—except my fertility." Since it distorts the language of the body, contraception is damaging and immoral.

In addition to violating the language of the body in sex, contraception violates the language of the body proper to masculinity and femininity. Male contraceptives violate the masculine call to protect the woman by communicating instead, "You need to be protected from me." Female contraceptives violate the welcoming aspect of femininity as they shun the whole man as well as the potential for life. Moreover, consider the language of the body proper to taking a pill. We take pills when something is wrong with our bodies and needs to be cured, i.e., medication. Therefore, taking birth control pills is akin to saying, "My fertility is a disease and needs fixing." A woman's fertility is one of God's greatest gifts and makes her uniquely feminine, yet society accuses, "Your femininity needs to be altered. We don't accept you completely."

For more background into contraception, we recommend Dr. Janet Smith's audio presentation *Contraception: Why Not?*

A related issue is the modern technology of creating new life without sex at all. Just as all sexual intimacy should be an expression of lifelong love, all babies deserve to come from love and be born into a lifelong family. Some technology separates sex and new life completely, showing that our acceptance of contraception (separating sex from openness to life) leads to things like in vitro fertilization. This is dangerous because it encourages us to think of babies as products we can create whenever we want them. Nobody—however small or young—should ever be considered a product. Thinking of people as products makes it very easy to start attaching human value to conditions, like health or beauty or intelligence or talent. Conditional value is a very dangerous way to understand the world—and nothing like the way God cherishes us just for being us.

Having said the above, proceed with sensitivity in presenting this teaching. Some of the youth you encounter may have been conceived by such technologies. They, like all human persons, are loved and willed into existence by God! A presentation of this teaching, without delicacy and compassion for any families involved with these technologies, could cause great hurt.

The Church teaches that family planning is wise and responsible for married couples. In order to care for their family best, a couple may experience legitimate reasons for avoiding pregnancy (e.g., family illness or serious financial hardship). When avoiding pregnancy becomes prudent, the Church encourages couples to use Natural Family Planning (NFP). NFP encompasses several highly effective methods in which the couple practices periodic abstinence during the woman's fertile phases. Unlike contraception, periodic abstinence during fertility in no way violates the language of the body in sex. In their sexual unions, the couple still gives themselves fully and do nothing to block the possibility of life.

The benefits of obeying God's design are manifold. Many couples who practice NFP report that they experience a "new honeymoon" each month as well as deeper intimacy stemming from ongoing communication. Perhaps most telling: The divorce rate of NFP users is somewhere between one and three percent.[1]

For more about Church teaching on family planning, see paragraphs 2366-2372 of the *Catechism*. For more about NFP, see www.usccb.org/nfp, www.nfpandmore. org, or www.ccli.org.

Is masturbation wrong? It doesn't hurt anybody.

Masturbation is touching your own body, particularly the sexual parts, to experience sexual pleasure. It often accompanies pornography and is just as counterproductive to real love. God designed the language of the body in sex to reveal complementarity and to bring about communion. Masturbation reduces sex from expressing total self-gift to expressing total self-centeredness. Masturbation trains us to use sex as just another form of pleasure or recreation. Imagine the damage caused in a relationship by such a selfish habit and a misuse of the body.

C.S. Lewis says that the man who masturbates forms in his imagination a "harem of brides" which makes no demands on him, and masturbation becomes a prison within himself that he begins to love.[2] It is hard to love another when we are in a prison we have made for ourselves.

For the person who understands this, acting out of selfishness can be gravely sinful. However, we must remember that full consent is necessary for the commission of a mortal sin. Sadly, many youth and adults have formed the habit of masturbation. Thus, their culpability may be diminished. If you present this to your group, remind them that, as we taught in Chapter 4, habits are hard to break. But we should never despair! Frequent reception of the sacrament of Reconciliation will both absolve sin and provide grace to conquer even the worst habit. For more information on this, see CCC 2353.

Is homosexuality wrong?

If you address this question, consider what is happening in the mind and heart of the asker. Many youth have family members or friends who have "come out of the closet," or they themselves may struggle with homosexuality. All desire and should be given love and compassion.

Members of Courage—a Catholic ministry to people struggling with same-sex attraction—caution that if we do not give a thorough, loving response to the question of homosexuality, some may perceive the Church as mean-spirited and bigoted. This is not a recommendation to avoid or water down the truth, but an emphasis that the topic must be broached delicately. This important and serious subject should never be joked about or ridiculed.

While same-sex attraction in itself is not immoral—only *acting* upon the attraction is immoral—it is nonetheless a serious disorder from God's design for sex. God made every person unique, unrepeatable, and worthy of love. In fact, love is the only proper response to any

---

[1]   *What's Wrong with Contraception?* (Cincinnati, OH: The Couple to Couple League International); Mercedes Arzú Wilson, "The Practice of Natural Family Planning Versus the Use of Artificial Birth Control: Family, Sexual, and Moral Issues," *Catholic Social Science Review* 7 (November 2002).

[2]   From a letter to a Mr. Masson dated March 6, 1956, in the Wade Collection at Wheaton College in Wheaton, Illinois.

human person. Nonetheless, the particular spousal love expressed by sexual union is to be shared between a man and woman. Marriage is the loving union of a man and a woman with the possibility of bringing children into the world. This is something that is impossible for two men or two women to achieve; therefore, they cannot be married. Friendship can be deep and personal, but the language of the body in friendship is not sexual activity. Thus, real love cannot support or encourage disordered same-sex attraction—even just an attraction—because following disordered passions of any kind prevents us from experiencing true happiness or fulfillment.

The Church has no definitive opinion on the origins of same-sex attraction. Regardless of why a person struggles with same-sex attraction, the Church teaches that fostering or acting upon the attraction must be avoided—a teaching motivated by the Church's loving desire to help everyone live in freedom and joy.

As mentioned above, God made every person unique, unrepeatable, and worthy of love. As Pope John Paul in his first encyclical states, "Man cannot live without love" (*Redemptor Hominis*, 10). Sexual desire itself was created to lead humanity to self-giving and life-giving relationships in marriage and family life. Some may therefore misinterpret Church teaching about homosexuality as callously barring those who struggle with same-sex attraction from expressing and receiving such love. Yet because the truth of the language of the body in sex depends upon the complementarity of a husband and wife's bodies, homosexual acts cannot express this meaning.

Amid the constant bombardment of misinformation about homosexuality, youth can be easily confused about their own feelings. Assure them that having close friendships with others of the same gender is good. Encourage anyone struggling with same-sex attraction to talk with a trusted adult. For resources, see paragraphs 2357-2359 in the *Catechism*. The ministries of Courage (for those struggling with same-sex attraction) and EnCourage (for family members and friends of those struggling with same-sex attraction) are online at www.couragerc.net.

About the Authors

Brian Butler is the co-founder and president of Dumb Ox Productions, Inc., a non-profit organization doing chastity and vocation formation for teens and young adults. He is co-author of *Theology of the Body for Teens: High School Edition* and the director of the feature-length reality film, *Mystery Trip*. Brian's bachelor's degree is in communications and he holds a master's degree in theology from Notre Dame Seminary School of Theology.

He served as the associate director for youth catechesis in the Archdiocese of New Orleans for two years, after spending five years teaching theology and coordinating campus ministry at the high school level. He has more than fifteen years of youth ministry experience and currently coordinates vocation formation initiatives for youth in the Diocese of Houma-Thibodaux and the Archdiocese of New Orleans. He and his wife, Lisa, reside in the New Orleans area with their four children.

Jason Evert is a best-selling author of a dozen books, including *Theology of His/Her Body* and *How to Find Your Soulmate without Losing Your Soul*. He also co-authored *Theology of the Body for Teens: High School Edition* along with his wife, Crystalina, and Brian Butler. Jason earned a master's degree in theology, as well as undergraduate degrees in counseling and theology, from the Franciscan University of Steubenville.

As full-time apologist with Catholic Answers, Jason has spoken internationally to more than a million teens about the virtue of chastity. He is a frequent guest on radio programs and his television appearances include Fox News, the BBC, MSNBC, and EWTN. Jason founded the website chastity.com, which is the homepage for his apostolate, The Chastity Project, which gives away more than 250,000 chastity resources every year to teens in more than forty countries.

Aimee and Colin MacIver currently teach theology at Saint Scholastica Academy in Covington, Louisiana, where Colin serves as the religion department chair and campus ministry coordinator. In addition to teaching in Catholic high schools, they have also served in various youth ministries for nearly ten years.

Colin travels nationally and internationally as a team member and speaker for Dumb Ox Productions bringing the message of purpose and purity to youth. Aimee previously worked as a public relations writer for Franciscan University of Steubenville. Colin holds a bachelor's degree in philosophy from Franciscan University of Steubenville and a master's degree in theology from Our Lady of Holy Cross College in New Orleans. Aimee has a bachelor's degree in communications from Franciscan University of Steubenville. The MacIvers welcomed their greatest endeavor when they adopted their first child, Leo, in the spring of 2010.

THEOLOGY OF THE BODY *for Teens*

HIGH-SCHOOL EDITION

A New Language for a New Generation

Theology of the Body for Teens presents the two hottest topics on the planet—God and sex—and "marries" them through Pope John Paul II's compelling vision for love and life. Using a great mix of stories, real-life examples, activities, prayers, and references to the culture that teens understand, *Theology of the Body for Teens* answers the questions teens have about their own bodies, issues on sexual morality, and how they were uniquely created for greatness.

Theology of the Body for Teens answers questions such as:

- Why did God give us our sexual desires?
- What is the difference between love and lust?
- What if I've already "messed up"?
- How far is "too far"?

- How can teens remain pure in our oversexed culture?
- Is there any hope for overcoming lust and pornography?

Review the Program Risk-Free!

Pastors, Educators, and Youth Ministers: Visit tobforteens.com or call 1-800-376-0520 for details.

Written and presented by Brian Butler and Jason & Crystalina Evert

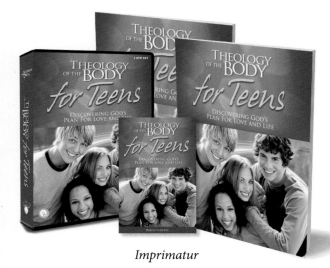

Imprimatur

Program Components Include:

- 4 DVD Set
- Student Workbook
- Leader's Guide
- Parent's Guide

What others are saying…

This study is put together masterfully! With all that teens face in today's world, this program is a must.

-Jeff Stankovsky
Director of Youth Ministry
St. Maria Goretti Catholic Church,
Indianapolis

I have seen tremendous fruit from this program. Before my eyes, I saw teens open up to a new vision of life and sexuality.

-Meaghan Weaver
Chastity Program Coordinator
Diocese of Palm Beach

Visit tobforteens.com for:

- *Leader's Training Videos*
- *Sample Chapters • Video Highlights*
- *Retreat Guide • Parent's Info Session Guide …and many more free downloads!*